Super-Nutrition
For
Dogs n' Cat

Preventive Medicine for your Pets

By
Nina Anderson
And
Dr. Howard Peiper

Safe Goods Publishing

•

SUPER NUTRITION
FOR DOGS N' CATS
by Nina Anderson and Dr. Howard Peiper

Copyright©2000 by Nina Anderson and Howard Peiper

All Rights Reserved

No part of this book may be reproduced in any form without the written
consent of the publisher

ISBN 1-884820-59-X
Library of Congress Catalog Card Number 00-132683
Categories: 1. Pets—Health   2. Veterinary—Nutrition
Printed in the United States of America

Edited by Arlene Murdock

Cover photographs by Jeanne Vuyosevich and Neil Shively

Super Nutrition for Animals for Dogs n' Cats is not intended as medi[
advice. It is written solely for informational and educational purpos[
Please consult a health professional should the need for one be indicat[
Because there is always some risk involved, the author and publisher a[
not responsible for any adverse effects or consequences resulting from the
use of any of the suggestions, preparations or methods described in this
book. The publisher does not advocate the use of any particular diet or
health program, but believes that the information presented in this book
should be available to the public.

*All listed addresses, phone numbers, and fees have been reviewed and up-
dated during production. However, the data is subject to change.*

Published by Safe Goods
283 East Canaan Rd.
East Canaan, CT 06024
(860) 824-5301

ACKNOWLEDGEMENTS:

We would like to thank all the animal lovers who contributed their knowledge in support of this work. The people who offered their humane stories are special, and we commend them for believing that they could find an alternative way to help their animals. We also thank the manufacturers of natural products that have made such a difference, not only in our lives, but in our pets' lives. We would like to express our gratitude to all the scientists, physicians, and researchers who have devoted vast amounts of time in discovering the benefits of nutrients in foods, nutritional supplements, and natural medicine.

We give our special thanks to Charlie Fox, Wakunaga Corporation. Without his support and knowledge, this book would not have been completed. Also, we give our gratitude to Jeanne Vuyosevich, Bill Pratt and Neil Shively for their heartwarming photographs and Modra Modrakowski for her artwork. We love our pets as special members of the family, and hope we have made the quality of their lives healthier and more enjoyable. We want to thank them for their trust.

photo by Neil Shively

3

FOREWORD

By Stephen Tobin, D.M.V., Meridan, CT
   Past President of The Holistic Veterinary Medical Association

In the past ten years, holistic medicine, both human and veterinary, has come a long way. Where holistic practitioners used to be regarded as quacks, they are now being referred clients by conventional practitioners. The most common question has gone from "is he a real doctor?" to "what modalities does he use?" and "how long must I wait to get an appointment?" Health insurers and HMO's are now encouraging alternative practices, as these save money for them by keeping their enrollees healthier. It is hard to read a magazine or watch TV without seeing an ad for some herbal product.

The real advantage of holistic medicine isn't that we can now substitute a plant steroid for a synthetic steroid, or use acupuncture or homeopathy instead of surgery. Its strength is that by maintaining a healthful situation, by avoiding those procedures and products that harm patients, human and animal, we can in many instances avoid illness. That is the advice that Nina Anderson and Dr. Howard Peiper have given in Super Nutrition for Dogs n' Cats. Homeopathy, acupuncture and chiropractic, in the hands of a trained, experienced person can cure disease, but the most important aspect of good health is avoiding disease in the first place. The emphasis in this book is first, to feed your pets properly to meet their nutritional needs. If you haven't been doing this, or think you have and your pet is sick anyway, this book gives very practical advice as to what you can do before you need to see a practitioner. If you do need to seek professional help, the authors discuss several treatment modalities you may want to consider.

The dreaded scourges of the past were mostly infectious diseases that have been overcome primarily by hygiene. The majority of illnesses we see today are chronic, degenerative diseases. One could almost view them as environmental diseases, as they are due to poisons in our foods (pesticides and herbicides), nutrients out of our foods (processing) and poisons bypassing our natural lines of defense (vaccinations).

In my professional opinion, in the last fifty years, the greatest damage to our pets' health, has been caused by vaccinations, and commercial pet food. Whenever someone tells me that they once had a dog that lived to be twenty years old, I ask them what they fed the dog. The response, in every single instance, was "whatever we ate", rarely "supermarket" dog food. This book will help you help your pet stay healthy.

Note: Dr. Tobin can be reached for phone consultations at his office in Connecticut: (203) 238-9863 (There is a charge for his expertise.)

INTRODUCTION

If you are in the mood for entertaining reading, then you can flip through this book and read the personal stories from folks just like you, who have found a way to heal their pet. If this is as far as you get, you will still receive valuable information. For those who truly want to improve the well being of their four-legged or winged family members, we have details on food, nutrition, healing supplements and manufacturers of healthy products that improve the immune system. This book is an updated version of Super Nutrition for Animals and our first book, Are You Poisoning Your Pets?

Veterinarians report that many of today's pets suffer from allergies, skin problems, hypertension, heart disease, cancer, liver and kidney failure, to name a few. These conditions have been exaggerated by the "tainted" foods we feed our pets, and the lack of vitamins, enzymes, minerals and other nutrients. There are approximately eighty million pet-owners in the United States. These animal lovers spend twenty-seven billion dollars on their pets and of that, eleven billion is on food. Advertising in the pet industry is the primary way you hear about their products. Do manufacturers tell you what they put in their cans or boxes? Is it a dead dog or cat? That may sound harsh, but for some manufacturers, it's true. "4D" is a FDA classification denoting a dead, dying, diseased and disabled meat source. Do they tell you what effect the preservatives and additives may have on your pets health? Of course not! All you see is happy healthy animals lapping up their "yummy" food.

Manufacturers of natural pet foods have lots more conscience. They have provided us with much of their research into what really should be in pet foods and what shouldn't. We have been made aware of the hazards of toxic additives and the need for specific nutrients. Unfortunately, even the most trustworthy natural pet food manufacturer must cook or process foods. Therefore, to restore the natural digestibility of the food, supplemental enzymes must be added to the meal. This is one of the focal points covered within the text. There are numerous good books on natural treatments for healing sick pets, and most mention diets, but we go one step further. Information is given on three important features: minerals, enzymes, and balancing nutrients.

To make our point, we have included numerous personal stories from pet owners about the healing power of diets, supplements, natural food and alternative treatments for illness. They are included not only to entertain you, but to help you make a more educated decision about the future health of your pet. Each story has key words underlined, depicting the animal species and the health problem that is the focus of the tale. This book is meant to be a starting point for you. Other sources are recommended within the text, to round out your education on specific topics. A Resource Directory is provided as the last chapter. It's purpose is to educate you about products and companies that are dedicated to keeping your pet alive and healthy, naturally. Should your animal be poisoned (from food or toxic substances) you can receive immediate help by calling the National Animal Poison Control Center (888) ANI-HELP (charge for service).

Our personal stories may not be as life threatening as those of the pet owners who sent us letters, but they illustrate our commitment to natural healing and preventive medicine.

→ *"When my cat Misty was eight years old, although she was full grown and seemingly healthy, she only weighed four pounds. When I wrote our first pet book, 'Are You Poisoning Your Pets?' I took my own advice and started feeding Misty premium cat food and supplements. I added minerals to her water and got rid of her toxic chemical flea collar, preferring to give her nutritional yeast and aged garlic extract supplements as flea prevention. She never did get fleas, even though she was an outdoor cat.*

One time, she was bitten. I knew she had an abscess beneath the skin, and called the vet to ask what his procedure was. For lots of money, he would lance the wound, put a drain in and give her antibiotics. For free, I applied a hot compress of sea salt and water every few hours until the abscess opened up (24 hours). I gave her Echinacea herbal drops diluted in water, with a syringe directly into her mouth, fed her a complex mineral, enzyme, vitamin, essential fatty acid and sea vegetable supplement, and mineral water every four hours. Once opened, the wound was treated with liquid aged garlic extract directly into the wound, and orally. I continued the supplements for ten days. The wound was completely drained within four days, and healed nicely. Once drained and closed, I applied Calendula ointment to the wound. She completely recovered, using old-fashioned home remedies, and I saved lots of money! Misty mysteriously went to sleep in the neighbors garage one day, never to wake up. I will always miss her.

Since Misty departed to that spiritual place, Bootsie appeared in the back yard. Full of worms, cuts, abscesses and generally looking like the typical stray alley cat, he bugged me until we took him in. A trip to the

vet revealed Bootsie had feline AIDS. Not one to let that deter me from giving him a good home, I started research into keeping him alive and healthy. Dr. Stephen Tobin, a holistic veterinarian, recommended that I administer homeopathic remedy specifically designed for the FIV virus. In addition I boosted his immune system by giving him home cooked foods and health-food pet food. He also received enzymes, minerals, flax, aci-dophilus, bee pollen, velvet antler, and a general vitamin supplement. Two years later, Bootsie is an 18-pound picture of health, and is joined by my four other stray cats, KiKi, Shadow, Sally and Buddy. (By the way, the sign on the door now says No Vacancy.)"
-Nina Anderson

Bootsie

→*"I had two dogs, a seven-year old greyhound, and a fourteen-year-old Brittany Spaniel. The Brittany had a grand mal seizure (epileptic) a year ago, and was near death. I started her on liquid crystalloid trace minerals (electrolyte form) as soon as she stopped shaking. Within one hour, she settled down and fell asleep. I have continued giving her various supple-ments, containing minerals, vitamins, greens, garlic, sea vegetables and essential fatty acids. I add enzymes to every meal I serve my dogs, and feed them only premium dog food or free-range meat scraps. I have found that supplementing her with minerals, nutritional yeast, flaxseed and lecithin has helped her retain her coordination, and she has not lost any brain function. The garlic seems to help with her arthritis, as I found this herb has excellent healing properties for joints. This regime also prevents flea infestations, which I'm sure she appreciates. Because of my care and the supplements she was given, she lasted two more years in a relatively pain-free state. We think of her often, and are using preventive methods to make sure our greyhound lives a long, long life."*
-Dr. Howard Peiper

TABLE OF CONTENTS

QUICK-REFERENCE REMEDY CHART

(H) = Herb   (C) = Homeopathic or Cell salt

	Arthritis	Bad breath	Blindness	Coat	Consti-pation	Cough
Alfalfa	X	X				
Anise (H)		X				X
Barley grass	X	X		X	X	
Bioflavanoid			X			X
Biotin				X		
Burdock (H)	X					
Boswella (H)	X					
Chlorophyll		X				X
Dandelion (H)	X					
Electrolytes	X	X	X	X	X	X
Enzymes	X	X		X	X	
Eyebright (H)			X			
Flaxseed	X		X	X	X	
Fenugreek (H)						X
Garlic		X		X	X	X
Horsetail (H)	X			X		
Magnets	X					
Marshmallow (H)						X
Minerals	X		X			X
Nat Mur (C)			X			
Nettles				X		
Nut. Yeast	X			X		X
Nux Vomica (C)					X	
Probiotics		X		X	X	
Royal Jelly				X		
St. Johns Wort (H)	X					
Tachyon	X			X		
Velvet antler	X					
Vitamin C	X			X		X
Vitamin A			X			
Wheat Grass	X	X			X	
Yucca (H)	X					

	Depression	Diarrhea	Digestion	Drippy Eyes	Dry skin	Fatigue
Alfalfa			X			
Aloe		X			X	
Aspen		X				
Barley grass		X	X		X	X
Bee Pollen						X
Bioflavanoid						X
Burdock					X	
Catnip (H)			X			
Electrolytes	X	X	X	X	X	X
Enzymes		X	X		X	X
Eyebright (H)				X		
Flaxseed	X		X	X	X	
Flower Remedies	X					
Garlic		X	X			
Horsetail (H)					X	
Kava Kava (H)	X					
Marshmallow (H)		X				
Magnets						X
Minerals	X	X	X			X
Nat. Mur (C)				X		
Nut. Yeast	X			X		X
Probiotics		X	X			
Red Clover (H)					X	
Rosemary (H)			X			
Slippery Elm (H)		X				
St.Johns Wort (H)	X					
Tachyon				X		X
Vitamin E				X		
Watercress (H)					X	
Wheat Grass		X	X		X	X

	Emotional Problems	Fleas	Fungus	Hip Dysplasia	Immune Support	Respiratory Ailments
Aloe						X
Barley grass			X	X	X	
Bioflavanoids				X	X	X
Biotin				X		
Boswella (H)				X		
Echinacea (H)						X
Electrolytes	X	X	X	X	X	X
Enzymes		X		X	X	
Flaxseed			X	X	X	
Flower Remedies	X		X			X
Garlic		X	X		X	X
Kava Kava (H)	X					
Magnets				X		
Minerals	X	X	X	X	X	X
Nut. Yeast		X			X	
Pennyroyal (H)		X				
Tea Tree Oil		X	X			
Valerian (H)	X					
Vitamin C				X		X
Wheat Grass		X	X		X	X

	Separation Anxiety	Urinary Problems	Worms
Alfalfa	X		
Aloe		X	
Barley grass	X		
Bearberry (H)		X	
Black Walnut (H)			X
Buchu (H)		X	
Cranberry		X	
Echinacea (H)		X	
Electrolytes		X	X
Enzymes		X	
Flower Remedies	X		
Garlic	X		X
Hawthorne (H)			X
Juniper		X	
Minerals	X	X	
Parsley		X	
SOD	X		
Southernwood (H)			X
Wheat Grass	X	X	X
Wormwood (H)			X

Household pets die younger now than ever before. Statistics show that the normal lifespan for the average pet dog or cat in the United States has decreased by approximately eighteen percent in the last forty years. The problem is that our pets are becoming nutritionally deficient, due to the fact that most commercial pet foods lack sufficient minerals, enzymes, and proper nutrients. Commercial-grade pet foods may contain harmful additives and processed grains, instead of high-quality proteins. These foods weaken the immune system, providing the environment for disease to gain a foothold.

Improving your pet's health is relatively simple. In this book you will learn about the importance of minerals, enzymes and essential fatty acids, and the part they play in prolonging the life of your pet.  Some animals are born with deficiencies of these important elements. This is often the result of a malnourished mother. Unfortunately, if the problem is not corrected in the present generation, each subsequent generation inherits a constitution weaker than the one before. A great example of this is a story you may be familiar with.

→ *Dr. Francis Pottenger studied six hundred cats in the 1930's. He fed these animals good quality beef, until the depression restricted his budget. Half of the cats were put on processed food. Although Dr. Pottenger did not plan to study the effects of this dietary change, he noted that the health of the animals in each group was markedly different. After three generations, the cats fed processed foods developed degenerative diseases, such as arthritis, in what would be their teen-age years. He deduced that this occurred because the food was enzyme-deficient, and the body had to work harder to digest the meals. As each animal became deficient, they had less enzymes to pass along to their offspring. Thus, the domino effect compromised the health of the newer generations.*

Having a good constitution is a major factor in our animal's ability to defend itself against disease. It is wise to prevent disease before it begins, and even an inherently weak constitution may be strengthened through gentle loving care and simple measures that enhance the immune system. This chapter will describe the basics needed by all animals (and humans), that keep their bodies functioning properly.

The basics include minerals, enzymes and essential fatty acids in the proper amounts from reliable sources. Without them our pets (and their owners) would die. Minerals that used to come to us in perfect balance through our food and drinking-water, now are missing or are delivered in a form that cannot be assimilated by the body. This is due to the soil being altered by modern farming methods, acid rain and other types of pollution. These nutritional basics can shore-up the old' immune factory and keep those trips to the vet minimal.

•MINERALS

On March 12, 1996, the New York Times reported that wild moose ingested excess concentrations of molybdenum from grazing on pastures where lime was spread to counteract the effects of acidification from rainfall. Excessive molybdenum created a copper deficiency, causing a toxic imbalance in the liver. This copper deficiency caused hundreds of moose to become emaciated. Their hair became discolored, and they suffered from osteoporosis, ulcers, diarrhea, convulsions, blindness and sudden heart failure. If mineral upset can have this disastrous effect in the wild, what are we doing to create similar imbalances in our pets?

Our favorite TV moose who appears in the opening credits of "Northern Exposure" also met his demise because of a mineral (cobalt and copper) deficiency in his diet. Normally, moose in the wild live to be sixteen, but fed in captivity by humans, life expectancy is only six or seven years. This may in part be due to a mineral deficiency or imbalance, created by inferior food products and polluted drinking water.

Minerals and trace elements must be present for growth, development and for all the body processes to work. If your pets are lucky enough to have a conscientious human caregiver, they will trust your judgment in supplying them with complete nutrition. This must include minerals, in the form of supplements added to their drinking water or food. The immune systems of animals have responded favorably to mineral treatment, with many sick pets receiving a speedy recovery. Stress, illness and environmental assaults can upset the mineral balance in our animals, creating many ailments, therefore, we must supplement our pet's diets (and our diets), with useable (by the body) minerals and electrolytes.

Mineral deficiencies may appear in pets as sickness or allergy. Lack of zinc, for instance, can cause vomiting, conjunctivitis, debility, and retarded growth in cats. Proper levels of zinc give skin and coat protection. Zinc also protects molecules and tissues against free radicals, thereby representing an essential component of antioxidant enzymes. Zinc is required for the activity of over 100 different kinds of enzymes in animal health. Calcium deficiencies in dogs result in osteoporosis, hip dysplasia, gum erosion and teeth loss, easily broken bones, and reproductive failures. In cats, symptoms are nervousness, lameness, thin bones and unfriendly behavior.

Copper deficiencies present symptoms such as loss of hair pigmentation and bone abnormalities. Low potassium contributes to muscle weakness, poor growth, listlessness, irregular heartbeat and lesions in the kidneys. Manganese deficiencies can contribute to reproductive dysfunction, weak tendons and ligaments, impaired bone formation, anemia, neuromuscular dysfunctions, and glandular swelling.

A similar unbalancing of minerals can occur with excessive intake of single vitamins, either by producing a deficiency or increasing the retention of a particular mineral. A high intake of vitamin C decreases copper's absorption and will contribute to a deficiency. Too much zinc can unbalance copper and iron levels in the body. Iron deficiencies can cause anemic conditions, weakness and fatigue.

Excess calcium, sometimes used for breeding and lactating females, can cause kidney failure and stones, as well as contributing to skeletal abnormalities and poor growth. In order to have the calcium absorbed, vitamin D, boron and magnesium must be present. Calcium, when balanced with magnesium, may actually *guard* against stones forming. The effect of calcium-magnesium imbalance has been seen in dairy cattle for years. A condition known as grass staggers exhibits symptoms such as unsteady gait, muscular twitching and uncontrollable flicking of their tail. Without enough magnesium to counterbalance the stimulating effect of calcium, muscles stiffen up or contract at will. The result may be cramps, irritability, twitching or even tremors. Drugs may deplete minerals, by increasing their excretion, or interfering with mineral imbalance.

All minerals must work together in the proper amounts. To maintain the delicate balance, it is therefore not wise to administer any singular mineral supplements without proper guidance. We, as owners, can also cause sickness in our pets, by playing doctor and administering single minerals without regard to their effect on other minerals, or on the body. As a maintenance procedure, add minerals to their diet through a properly balanced trace-mineral supplement. This will assure that their bodily functions operate properly, that their antioxidant enzymes are strong to fight infections, and that their immune systems stay strong. The following story depicts one success of treatment with combination mineral supplements.

→ *"At the tender age of eight years, our dog, Heidi began displaying the classical symptoms of Hip Dysplasia. Our next door neighbor, a woman who was originally a registered nurse, and now a D.V.M., informed me that Heidi had the onset of severe Hip Dysplasia. She felt the best I could do was to put Heidi to sleep, as there is no known cure for this problem. Shortly thereafter, I saw a couple who were patients of mine, and who ran a dog kennel for many years. I told them of my quandary regarding our beloved Heidi.*

They mentioned that there was experimental research being done at a major veterinary school in Scotland and that they would make inquiry. Several weeks later I received a very big package of research material on Hip Dysplasia. It disclosed two major areas of concern. The quantity of calcium in the body and the absorption factors regarding this calcium. I recalled from my naturopathic training, that all animals and humans have the same basic nutritional needs. I immediately started supplementing her diet with a good calcium-magnesium citrate, and most important of all, a true electrolyte solution.[1]

After several weeks, I began to notice subtle improvements in my dog, such as standing easier and walking straighter. Suffice to say that within several months, my eight-year-old Heidi became a puppy again, no longer looking like the tired, old aching dog she was! Many years later, at the ripe old age of sixteen, our beloved Heidi was laid to rest. We are now retired, and maintain a small organic farm in Florida with our Heidi 'Two'. She is eight years old, and has no signs of that horrible disease. We supplement her diet with electrolytes as a major aid in calcium absorption, and several additional nutrients."
Dr. I. (Gerald) Olarsch, N.D., Florida

---

[1] Pet-Lyte, by Nature's Path.

→ *"I recently received a story from a woman who has a Boxer, male. He caught Parvo from the vaccination, when he was six weeks old. When the diarrhea started, she immediately tried an electrolyte supplement[2]. He never developed a fever and never vomited, but ultimately had to have major intestinal surgery and three blood transfusions, his spleen and a few other things done, all by the age of nine weeks. Because of the supplement, he never got dehydrated!*

After the surgery, the vet called and told her to come and pick him up and take him home, because no other dog in the country has survived this type of surgery, and it would be better if he died at home. She again started the electrolyte formula right away, and the vets were shocked at his total and complete recovery. He is now three years old, and has one major and two single points towards his championship. Everyday is a miracle for him, and without the electrolytes, she doesn't think he would have survived!"

-Janis Gianforte, New Jersey

If you think you can feed your animals mineral-rich vegetables, think again! Obtaining minerals from vegetable sources is becoming more difficult each year due to non-organic farming methods and acid rain, which lowers the pH of the soil. Starved for trace minerals, plants now take up toxic pesticides, fertilizers and 'bad' minerals. One such mineral, aluminum, has caused cats to suffer from a lack of coordination, rabbits to develop memory problems, and birds to lay eggs with fragile shells. Food processing further depletes the needed micronutrients in our food. Symptoms of deficiencies include coat, skin, and allergy problems, breeding and growth difficulties, weakened immune systems and a general lack of thriftiness. Giving your animal premium pet foods or supplements are necessary to correct any deficiencies.

Although many minerals supplements are balanced and safe, they are not all alike in their ability to be utilized by the body. Though a supplement may contain a dozen different minerals, the question is—"in what form are those minerals being offered?" Colloidal minerals are larger and are less likely to be completely absorbed. Chelated food-source minerals (bound with an amino acid) are smaller, and therefore better absorbed by the body. Ionic minerals are smaller yet. Crystalloid minerals are the smallest, and more likely to be one hundred percent absorbed. A crystalloid is a

---

[2] Nupro Custom Electrolyte Formula by Nutri-Pet Research.

substance, like a crystal, which forms a true solution and can pass through a living membrane. Minerals, when they are electrically charged and found in solution, contain electrolytes (electrical charge necessary for life). These electrolytes are necessary for life, and the more active your pet is, the more they need to replenish the electrolytes lost through sweat (panting) and muscle use.

The safest and best way to help your pet is to add a complete mineral supplement to its diet. These should include the trace-minerals such as organic copper, zinc, chromium, selenium, and iodine, micronutrients, plus certain macro-minerals (those needed in large amounts) that form the electrolytes which carry out all bodily functions. Liquid products are convenient, as they can be dribbled into purified water and given to all types of animals. Supplements can be also be offered in pill form, or as powdered nutrients to mix with food. What follows is a personal account of a pet owner who gave trace mineral supplements to her cat, and experienced great results.

→ *"I have a seven-year-old cat by the name of Chancy. She was a show cat for many years, and was given to me by the old owner who raised Persians. While I was on vacation, I gave her to a family member to take care of. When I returned, we found that Chancy had developed a bladder infection. The vet bill came to over $600., and although she made progress, the condition returned a few weeks later.*

When I again contacted the vet, he suggested additional treatment. I could not afford to spend more money, so I asked the woman who had initially given us the cat, if she had an alternative solution. She suggested that I put Chancy on a liquid mineral supplement[3]. The next morning I put seven drops in Chancy's water, and continued in this manner for the next few days. Soon after, I began to notice a change in her personality. She became playful and lively, like she had been as a kitten. Ever since then, a day has not passed that I have not given her the mineral supplement. Her infection went away, and we have never had a problem since."
-Lisa LeFebvre, Florida

---

[3] Pet-Lyte,™ by Nature's Path.

The following list depicts the function of certain minerals.

- **Calcium:** Bone formation, muscle contraction, metabolism, blood clotting, bone strength.
- **Chloride:** Kidney function, Fluid and acid/alkaline balance.
- **Chromium:** Guards against cardiovascular disease.
- **Copper:** Enables incorporation of iron into hemoglobin. Bone & cartilage formation.
- **Fluorine:** Important in bone and teeth development.
- **Iodine:** Constituent of thyroxin for thyroid function, control of metabolism, growth and reproduction.
- **Iron:** Constituent of hemoglobin. Cell metabolism.
- **Magnesium:** Inter-related to calcium and phosphorus for development of bones. Assists metabolism, protein synthesis, nerve excitability and energy production on a cellular level.
- **Manganese:** Assists metabolism of carbohydrates, protein and fats. Calcium and phosphorus utilization, bone development, reproduction and fertility.
- **Pantothenic Acid** is necessary for iron to be incorporated into hemoglobin.
- **Phosphorus:** Assists with metabolism and bone growth.
- **Potassium:** Inter-related to sodium in nerve and muscular function. Balances fluid and cellular metabolism.
- **Selenium:** Inter-related with vitamin E as an antioxidant. Contained in enzyme glutathionine peroxidase, which protects muscle membranes.
- **Sulfur:** Amino acids methionine and cysteine.
- **Zinc:** Assists metabolism, forms cartilage and hoof. Maintains hair, skin health.

•ENZYMES

The next element in the body's line of defense is enzymes, those mysterious forces that convert substances in our body to useable nutrients. A body cannot make its own minerals, but it does have the power to make enzymes. They are activated, energized protein molecules, and can be thought of as the construction workers in the body, that build the structure and keep it repaired. There are three primary groups of enzymes: *metabolic enzymes* that catalyze various chemical reactions within the cells, such as detoxification and energy production; *digestive enzymes* that are secreted along the gastrointestinal tract to break down food, allowing nutrient absorption; and *antioxidant enzymes*, which assist in fighting free-radicals and viruses.

Unfortunately, a body can only call upon its enzyme reserves once in a while without overworking the pancreas. Enzymes that are used up in the digestion of food cause the enzyme storage banks to become depleted. Raw food contains its own enzymes necessary for digestion. When pets chew either raw food or prey, enzymes from that food are activated. After this initial pre-digestion, the food moves to the upper stomach where it continues to break down, remaining in this location for an hour before gastric secretions move in. At this point, the enzymatic action is disabled by the acids and doesn't kick in again until the food reaches the small intestine, where pH is more alkaline. Every raw food contains exactly the right amount and types of enzymes to digest that particular food. Cooked food contains no live enzymes. It is therefore a problem to feed pets cooked and processed food day in and day out.

If not enough enzymes are produced, then the food won't digest properly, and not only could your pet get a stomach ache, but other effects of maldigestion could appear in the form of food allergies. The pancreas can produce digestive enzymes to digest the cooked food, although it was not designed to work overtime. Eventually, the pancreas loses the ability to make enzymes, and degenerative disease sets in, as depicted by the following story.

→ *"We discovered our dog, Chief, had lymph cancer last fall. Having lost a dog to this same thing a number of years ago, we knew or thought we knew the horrible outcome. However, our veterinarian suggested an extensive chemotherapy treatment that included asparaginase vincristine, cytoxin and other chemotherapy drugs. He started his treatments in November. When Chief was three weeks into the treatment, he was extremely sore. He was so bad that he could not get up without crying, and needed help getting up. It was at this time Dr. Peterson gave us a small bottle of enzymes, remarking at the time that he really did not know what it did, but it seemed to help.*

We started giving him the enzymes,[4] along with his regular dog food and a special 'chicken stew' we had started feeding him prior to the chemotherapy treatments. Not only were we amazed, but we were extremely happy when we noticed, a few days later, he was getting up by himself, with only an occasional whimper. He also was moving better when we took him for his morning and evening walks. Not that he needed any complications, but arthritis had begun to be noticed last summer.

Chief is now in his final week of treatment, a five-day series of intravenous antibiotics. He acts like there had never been anything wrong with him. Anyone not seeing him when he was so excessively stiff and

---

[4] Prozyme,™ a powdered organic enzyme supplement.

sore, would not believe he had been in that condition seeing him now. In fact, a friend of ours who had seen him when he was so bad, could not believe the remarkable change.

Another item of note; prior to the start of his chemotherapy, Chief had lost approximately 15 pounds. He was normally a lean, trim 100 pounds, being taller and longer than the standard German Shepherd, so at 85 pounds he looked skinny. His weight gain started in December, right in the middle of chemotherapy treatments. From what we understand about that type of treatment, this is not the normal occurrence. Needless to say, his weight gain did not hurt our feelings whatsoever.

We learned that enzymes would help retard hair loss. It certainly did that. The only hair loss Chief suffered was his whiskers, the longer hairs above the eyes and a couple of thin spots above one eye. The whiskers and longer hairs above the eyes are growing back. At present they are approximately half their normal length and the thin spots are filling in as well.

We certainly wish we had known of the benefits of enzymes in the past. We most likely would have had some of our dogs and cats that have died, with us longer than they were."
-Lee & Sharon, Spokane, WA

Enzymes can't work alone and most require the presence of vitamins and minerals in order to do their work. For example, vitamins A, D, E, and K require fat for absorption and in order to be broken down, they need the enzyme, lipase. If supplies of this enzyme are deficient, fat will not be digested and absorbed properly, and the vitamins will not be released. Water-soluble vitamin- B's and C, also help enzymes do their job. Vitamin C is necessary for the enzyme that helps make collagen, a major component of skin. Minerals and electrolytes are necessary, because they are part of the enzyme structure. So you see, if enzymes are not present, the vitamins and minerals have no reason to be in the body.

There are no synthetic enzymes. Only living matter can produce them and because plant enzymes work in a wider range of pH found in the digestive tract, they are better all around enzymes than animal-based types. Adding plant enzymes to your pets' diet helps their food to be assimilated. This facilitates the repair of organs, glands, bones, muscles and nerves. Any excess is stored in the liver and the muscles. Like any addition to the body, introduce enzymes slowly, so your pet's body can make the proper adjustment to the extra help being given. The following stories are testimonials to the effectiveness of enzymes as a building block of the immune system.

→ *"Sara Bone is an Old English Sheep Dog who is now twelve years old, going on five! Sara is very happy and healthy, but unfortunately was not always this way. Several years ago, Sara developed a very serious skin disorder. She had red pustules on her stomach and scaly, scabby sores on her back, which bothered her so much she was tearing her hair and skin off for relief.*

We took Sara to our local (well-respected) veterinarian, who immediately injected her with steroids and prescribed antibiotics and oral steroids which would "make her comfortable and heal the wounds." After about a year on both medications, her condition remained basically unchanged. As soon as the medication was decreased, the skin erupted again. Meanwhile, Sara's blood count was horrible, and the vet was concerned that he may have to operate because of her spleen. He felt that her immune system was unable to fight off whatever was causing the skin problem, so he started her on weekly injections of something that I believe he called SPL.

As you can imagine, Sara felt horrible. By the time she was eight-and-a-half years old, she appeared truly geriatric and was hardly able to walk around the block. I called the University of North Carolina Veterinary School to see if there was a 'doggie dermatologist' there that would take a look at her. They said they would start by placing her on a hypoallergenic diet for about ten weeks, and then test her for allergies, but they needed a recommendation from my vet to proceed. My veterinarian was outraged that I would take my pet somewhere else, and would not give me the referral. I decided to take matters into my own hands.

I discontinued the antibiotics and shots, and weaned her off the steroids. I developed my own dog food recipe which includes fresh and frozen veggies, legumes, organic brown basmati rice, non-fat cheese, virgin olive oil, garlic and other spices and grains. I added a barley grass juice powder[5], containing thousands of enzymes. Sara Bone now jogs half a mile every morning, and can hardly sit still. Her skin is clear, her coat is shiny and healthy. Her eyes have the whitest whites and her toes (which were almost devoid of hair), had the hair grow back and she stopped chewing on them. Sara no longer scratches all the time. We thought that

---

[5] Barley Dog™ by Green Foods Corp.

the diet change might be solely responsible, until I ran out of the powder and Sara went a week without! After the scratching and reappearance of a red pustule on her chest, I am pleased to know that she is back on the barley grass juice powder."
-Lori E., North Carolina

→ *"We have been using digestive enzyme supplements[6] for approximately one year now, and the difference in our eight year old Siberian Husky is remarkable, to say the least. About a year ago, we were dealing with a completely different animal. He could barely walk, and it was impossible for him to climb up our stairway at night to our bedroom. We had a complicated dilemma, in that he would not sleep anywhere other than by my side. If I fell asleep in my daughter's room at night, he would invariable find me in there, and I would awaken in the morning to find him sleeping next to me on the floor. When I moved from my daughter's room at night back into our own bedroom, he would follow. When the hip dysplasia became worse, he reached a point where he could not climb the stairs at all. He would lay at the bottom of the stairs and whine insufferably for hours.*

We couldn't carry him up the stairs because of his weight, and because we were fearful of it causing even greater harm to him. I tried sleeping downstairs at night to bring him some comfort, but that was NOT a long-term solution.

He was only seven years old when this problem became so bad I decided to reach out for help. Our veterinarian suggested costly shots and possibly surgery, which we didn't believe, was a viable solution to the problem. Our vet also recommended giving him multiple doses of aspirin throughout the day, and increasing it at night. The aspirin showed no sign of relieving any of his discomfort. He got tired of sleeping downstairs by himself, and devised a way of creeping up the stairs at night, by turning around and moving up the stairway backwards. He would sit down on his bottom and then use his front legs to balance himself, while he would slowly raise his back legs up to the next step, then sit down again and do it all over again. This took an insufferable amount of time, and was terrible to watch each evening. We'd all give a sigh of relief each night as he made it up one more time, and wondered how long we would be able to watch him continue to suffer in this way.

---

[6] Prozyme™ organic powdered plant enzymes.

One afternoon, I found myself turning to TV-38, a religious station in our area, to see a video of another Siberian Husky with hip dysplasia. I watched, before my eyes, the video of his improvement from the previous video. The product that they had been using was an enzyme supplement,[7] so we decided to try it to see if it could possibly make a difference. I am writing to tell you that our Husky now trots up the stairs at night, and even several times during the day. In the past, he would never go upstairs except at night, even if we were up there for long periods of time, because of the difficulty. Now if we go up, he goes up. And I recently spent a weekend afternoon with him in our backyard, watching him run and play as if he were a pup again. What a blessing this product has been in our lives. Believe me when we say enzymes were an answer to our prayers."
-Michael & Elizabeth Grinn, Illinois

•HEALING FATS

The third building block for a strong immune system is fat. It has been thought that fat people and fat pets need to go on low-fat diets. There are even low fat pet foods, but what we tend to overlook is the importance fats have in our bodies. It is not fat that that throws our bodies out of balance, but the type of fat that we eat. Unhealthy fats add cholesterol and excess weight. Good fats help us live longer and include the Omega 3 (EPA and DHA, alpha-linolenic) and Omega 6 (linoleic) essential fatty acids (EFA's). Without adequate stores of them, our cellular neurotransmitters break down, and send erroneous signals throughout the body. EFA's are not manufactured by the body (in humans or animals), therefore we must depend on food to supply these nutrients. An example follows in this story:

→ *"My dog, Nikki was diagnosed with pancreatitis. The vet was saying how bad she was, and nothing could be used to control her pain and symptoms, because she was highly sensitive to all medications. We were afraid that putting her down would soon be our only option. I was scared and extremely upset, to say the least! I searched out every book store I could find in southern California to find the older herbal and Chinese medicinal remedy books. In them I found specific references to symptoms which resembled Nikki's, and the use of olive oil and alfalfa.*

---

[7] Prozyme™ digestive plant enzymes.

28

I put her on alfalfa and olive oil daily, and continued that for the rest of her life. The recommendations in those books turned the situation around and gave her the relief she needed to help her system recover to a point where we could mostly control her bouts of pain and illness. The vet was quite surprised with what I was doing, and the positive results we obtained."
-Dawn Hoffman, Ohio

Dogs and cats need less oil than humans, but must depend on us to feed them essential fatty acid fortified food. Many pet food manufacturers use too few EFA's in their recipes. Oils will become rancid if exposed to oxygen, therefore manufacturers are reluctant to add them to their formulas. Instead, they choose to add refined (heated), non-organic high EFA oils such as corn. Heat processing limits the potential for rancidity, but also kills most of the complementary nutrients in the oils.

Many pet foods only contain one type of EFA, causing an imbalance and creating further deficiencies. For instance, if Omega 6 is not balanced by Omega 3, the arachidonic acid in the Omega 6 can get out of hand. Normally required for cellular growth, if left unchecked, this can create an overabundance of growth cells. If these cells are cancerous, then the situation could be life threatening. (Recent studies have shown that garlic can have a tempering effect on cellular overgrowth caused by this type of EFA imbalance.) Essential fatty acids are bioavailable (absorbable) to the body when in the complement of "minor" nutrients such as phytosterols, lecithin, vitamin E, and carotene The refining and heat extraction methods normally used, depletes the oils of these nutrients. Cold extraction methods are far superior and leave most oils as nature had intended. Flax oil, (Omega 3), sunflower and sesame seed oil (Omega 6) are good combination.

Oil supplements must be chosen carefully. Flax meal containing fiber, amino acids, and other nutrients for metabolism is a good choice, and easy to mix into food. Bottled oils are excellent if they are cold extracted, organic, are in a dark bottle and have been kept away from light, which can promote rancidity once the bottle is opened.

Warning: Flax oil, although wonderful for humans, can cause oxidative damage to tissues in cats and dogs, if given without the complementary "minor" nutrients mentioned above.

Essential fatty acids must be synthesized in the body; this requires Biotin, an essential B-vitamin that works as a nutritional enzyme for the synthesis of fatty acids. Biotin also helps metabolize carbohydrates and proteins, maximizing the nutritional value of your pet's diet. Certain common practices destroy this vitamin, such as chlorinating water (found in most city tap waters), which inactivates biotin. Biotin is also destroyed by rancidity from fat, (a common hazard of storing opened cans of food for a period of time), meat by-products and avidin, a substance found in raw egg whites. Pet foods listing eggs as an ingredient may contain avidin. Antibiotics and sulfonamides may decrease the natural intestinal synthesis of biotin; therefore, pets on these medications should definitely be given biotin and vitamin E supplements. Biotin supplements should also be included in your pet's food to prevent the loss of bioavailability of essential fatty acids.

The enzyme lipase also must be present to break down fats and make them useful to the body. If your pet's levels of enzymes are depleted due to a cooked food diet, as found in all processed pet foods, the essential fatty acids and other fats will not be digested. Plant enzyme supplements should be added to your animal's cooked food diet for this reason, among others stated previously in this chapter.

Given the proper balance of essential fatty acids, you will soon notice your pet's coat becoming thick and shiny. EFA's are extremely beneficial to skin and hair and can appear as a miracle cure. Dry flaky skin, increased cutaneous infections and hair loss in animals, is a good indication of EFA deficiencies. Many natural supplements found in the marketplace today contain the proper complement of EFA's, along with the 27 essential nutrients required for oil metabolism. The results produced include: the ceasing of excessive shedding; disappearance of feline acne and hair balls; improvement of doggy odors; drippy eyes and tear stained faces; elimination of dry skin, eczema, hot spots and oily skin; re-growth of hair; increased energy levels; reduction in symptoms of hip dysplasia; digestive problems lessened, and greater performance and stamina. The following letter illustrates the success of one of these multi-nutrient supplements containing EFA's.

→ *"I have owned dogs for twenty-five years and have been active in hunting, obedience, confirmation and agility. A year ago, we fenced in a new section of our property next to the woods and fields. The dogs were busy investigating, eating grass, digging holes and eating dirt. I am employed by a local animal hospital, and test my dogs for parasites yearly. The results have always been negative.*

Their last stool exam showed eggs unlike anything I'd ever seen before. The hospital doctors could not confirm what they were, and so a sample was sent to the lab for analysis. Results showed hooks, coccidia and round worms in all three of my dogs. None of them had ever had any parasites before. The interesting point was that none of these eggs looked normal, and they were unidentifiable by us at the hospital. Why? They appeared much smaller, and incompletely formed. Also, none of my dogs showed any ill health. All had normal stools and were in excellent coat, high energy, normal appetites, etc.

We had been using a vitamin supplement full of EFA's [8] for several months and the dogs were thriving on it. I feel very strongly that the formulas that were high in flaxseed interfered with the development of these parasites and prevented serious illness. Had I been feeding them this supplement before they had a six month start in the dirt, perhaps they would not have developed parasites at all."

-Cheryl Whitmore, New Jersey

3→ *"Our seventeen-plus year old Siamese cat, Pyewacket, was as one neighbor kindly put it, "on her last legs." The veterinarian said she had outlived her organs. My father assumed she'd be gone by Labor Day. My sister recommended I give her a supplement containing a long list of vitamins, minerals and essential fats.[9] I did, and within a week, Pyewacket's appetite was amazingly improved, and she was drinking water regularly again. Her legs are stronger, and she jumps to her favorite sofa inside, and her perch on the table outside. Her voice is stronger (the only improvement we could have done without, as she tends to exercise it in the middle of the night), and she has rejoined her friends in play. This supplement rich in essential fatty acids, is the only new addition to her regime, and it sure has improved the quality of her life."*

-Muff Singer, California

→ *"We now view fatty acids not as just 'supplements', but essential components of good health—essential fatty acids are needed to maintain healthy skin and coat, a strong heart and nervous system, and to build resistance to flea bites and other allergens. Most commercial diets, and many home-prepared diets, lack the quantity and diversity of Omega-3 and Omega-6 fatty acids, needed by dogs and cats to maintain vibrant health. I have used an EFA supplement[10] that provides a balanced array*

---

[8] NUPRO, high in flaxseed by Nutri-Pet Research.
[9] Missing Link, from Designing Health, Inc.
[10] Animal Essentials, Merritt Naturals

of EFA-rich vegetable and marine oils that our dogs and cats need. This supplement is contained in a hassle-free, twist-open, gel cap that keeps the oils fresh and makes feeding fun, because the gel cap looks like a fish. My dogs and cats love the formula, and their coats look great".

-Gregory Tilford, Author of "All You Ever Wanted To Know About Herbs for Pets."

Fifty-four million dogs and sixty-three million cats in the United States eat primarily what their owners give them. Many do not have a choice. If left to their own devices, most cats and dogs would eat differently out in the wild. Do they know something we don't? Do they really care that pet foods look appealing? Of course, they are attracted by smell, but certain ingredients may not be good for them. They eat it anyway because they have no alternatives. Providing them with fresh meat from the grocery store may not be the best choice either. Hormones and drugs are administered to feedlot animals on a regular basis. FDA regulations state that ten days before slaughter (or before *human* consumption), antibiotic therapy must cease. Are our inspectors enforcing these regulations? Do these "pollutants" end up in the flesh of these feed lot animals and in the meat that you give to your animals? If you prefer to put together your pet's dinner, choose free-range or organically-fed meat sources.

Pet food manufacturers are allowed to use this same meat, plus road-kill, diseased and pus-laden animals, euthanized pets, all labeled "by-products." Also included in pet food are turkey and chicken gullets. They are full of indigestible and potentially harmful materials, such as gravel and stones, which can cause diarrhea and blockages in dogs and cats. Metal bands on poultry are not normally removed before processing, and therefore can find their way into your pet's dinner. Also, sometimes found in canned pet food are the identification tags from euthanized pets—a horrible, but realistic eye opener to the lack of control in what goes in your cat or dog's dinner. Natural pet food manufacturers are aware of the hazards of "tainted" foods, and go to great lengths to avoid these meat sources.

We start off this chapter by letting you know what ingredients many manufacturers add to pet foods. You must be avid label readers if you are going to avoid veterinary bills. Pet foods may contain not only preservatives and additives, but the actual food may contain pus, fecal matter, road kill, viruses, cancerous tumors, infected blood, rancid fillers and bacteria. These by-products, according to Dr. P.F. McGargle, a veterinarian who has also served as a federal meat inspector, "can include moldy, rancid or spoiled processed meats, as well as tissue too severely riddled with cancer to be eaten by people." Dr. Alfred Plechner, D.V.M. comments on by-products, stating that "diseased tissue, pus, hair, assorted slaughterhouse rejects, and carcasses in varying stages of decomposition, are sterilized with chemicals, heat and pressure procedures." In some cases, additional processing with chemical sprays also occurs. Pet food may also contain many of the preservatives, fillers and additives that go into our food, but that does not make them healthy for your pet. The most common additives or harmful ingredients are listed below:

•NASTY FOOD ADDITIVES

ALUMINUM: In 1893, the Public Health Department in Bern, Switzerland warned that "damage to health from the consumption of food or drink from aluminum is to be expected". The Hahnmann Chronic Disease list included 1,160 verified symptoms of aluminum poisoning, including infertility, disorders of the blood, skin, nervous, glandular and digestive systems. Cats under the influence of aluminum suffered from a lack of coordination. Aluminum can contribute to diseases similar Alzheimer's, (thought to be an affliction of aluminum toxicity). Aluminum, in the body, will result in an "electrolyte imbalance" and disrupt vital body functions, leading to disease conditions. Animals thought to be aluminum "poisoned" should be treated with large amounts of trace minerals and vitamin C, good chelating agents which help to cleanse the body of this toxin.

Do you serve your pet water in an aluminum bowl? Does their pet food contain aluminum baking powder? Do you wrap scraps of food in aluminum foil? Does your water supplier add aluminum sulphate (a dirt-removing agent) to your water? Does your pet food contain plants grown organically in mineral rich soil? If not, the plant may be ingesting aluminum in place of needed minerals. This condition may be due to the fact that acid rain causes the good minerals to wash away, leaving behind the heavy metals. Although you don't intentionally give your pet aluminum, many of their symptoms may be attributed to this element, which they get through the water, air and food.

ANIMAL/ POULTRY FAT: Those scraps of meat which are not fit for human consumption go into pet foods. These rancid fats are heavily preserved with chemicals such as BHT/BHA and Ethoxyquin to prevent further spoilage. Fats in this form are difficult to digest and can lead to a host of health problems including diarrhea, gas, bad breath and vomiting. If fed to young animals, it can permanently affect the sensitive lining of the digestive tract leading to a lifetime of assimilation problems and allergic responses.

ARTIFICIAL COLOR: Most people are aware of toxic side effects of artificial colors and flavors from coal tar derivatives such as Red #40, a possible carcinogen, and Yellow #6, which causes sensitivity to fatal viruses in animals.

BHT/BHA: These petroleum products are used to stabilize fats in foods. In the process of metabolizing BHA and BHT, chemical changes occur in the body. These changes have caused reduced growth rate, and they inhibit white blood cell stimulation. In humans, they exhibit reactions such as skin blisters, hemorrhaging of the eye, weakness, discomfort in breathing, the reduction of the body's own antioxidant enzyme, glutathione peroxidase, and may cause cancer.

ETHOXYQUIN: This was originally designed as a rubber stabilizer and herbicide, and before its approval, the FDA characterized it as a poison. It was first introduced as a grain preservative on feed intended for animals raised for slaughter, and not expected to live more than two years. It has been reported to cause liver cancer in dogs, and can cause increased mortality and malformations in newborn puppies. It can contribute to skin allergies and some immune-related diseases.

MEAT BY-PRODUCTS: Called "4D" sources, this type of labeling on pet foods can contain, meat, tissues and insides of animals that are dead, dying, disabled or diseased, and not fit for human consumption when they reach the slaughterhouse. This translates to hooves, hides, hair, bones, feathers, beaks, and also can include euthanized pets and road kill. Feeding food that includes these wastes increases the animals' chance of getting cancer and other degenerative diseases, not to mention promoting cannibalism. (Mad Cow Disease is thought to be the cannibalistic result of including sheep and cow meat in cow feed, leading to the eventual disintegration of the brain.) Hormones, steroids and antibiotics in slaughtered animals are active even in "dead" tissues. Some by-products may be a good source of nutrition for your pet, such as organ meats, bones, skin, etc. Unfortunately, because government regulations dictate that the nutritional *and* 4D ingredients must all be labeled by-products, you really are unable to determine exactly what kind of "by-products" are in your food.

PEANUT HULLS: An inexpensive bulk-producing source of fiber, that can create chronic constipation and damage the tissues of the colon.

PESTICIDES: A must to maintaining a healthy diet is to avoid pesticides. Found just about everywhere, they are altering our genetic makeup, producing animal and bird mutations, and assuring eventual demise of the planet. Most obvious is the assault to health, manifesting itself as cancer. The Environmental Protection Agency now considers many previously approved chemicals to be potentially carcinogenic: 60% of all herbicides, 90% of all fungicides and 30% of all insecticides currently being used on our farm crops. A list of fruits and vegetables that are most susceptible to contamination from pesticides (unless you choose organic varieties) is listed in order of highest risk of contamination: strawberries, bell, green and red peppers, spinach, cherries, peaches, cantaloupe (from Mexico), celery, apples, apricots, green beans, grapes, cucumbers.

PROPYLENE GLYCOL: Used as a de-icing fluid for airplanes, this chemical is added to food and skin products to maintain texture and moisture, as well as inhibiting bacteria growth in the product. It also inhibits the growth of friendly bacteria in the digestive system by decreasing the amount of moisture in the intestinal tract, leading to constipation and cancer. It can affect the liver and kidneys.

SALT: Added as a preservative, salt can irritate the stomach lining, cause increased thirst, and aggravate heart and kidney problems through fluid retention. It can also increase blood pressure.

SODIUM NITRITE: Used in the curing of meats, this substance participates in a chemical reaction in the body that becomes carcinogenic. It is used also in pet foods to add color.

SOYBEAN: Pet food manufacturers add soybean to increase protein content and bulk. The form most prevalent is the unsprouted bean, which is very difficult to digest and assimilate because it contains enzyme inhibitors that prevent digestion of the soybean. Minerals assume the role of "digestor", which facilitates a loss of minerals from the body. This results in mineral-deficient diseases surfacing. The number one allergy in dogs is soy (the number two is wheat, three is corn). Side-effects of diets high in soy content are evident in animals after surgery, because the stitches don't hold well and infections set in more easily. The soy has compromised the immune system by reducing the levels of necessary minerals (electrolytes).It is the number one allergic food for dogs, and can lead to bloat, which is a major killer. Wild dogs must know this, as they do not touch soybeans in the field.

SUGAR AND OTHER SWEETENERS: The most common sweeteners in pet foods are beet sugar, corn syrup, molasses and sucrose. They are used as preservatives, and have the side-effect of creating sugar addicts in pets. They require almost no digestion, and are rapidly absorbed into the blood stream. These will provide sugar highs, (just as humans experience) and subsequent lows, inhibit the proper growth of friendly intestinal bacteria, and slow down the digestive system while being processed, limiting nutrient absorption. Sugar can also contribute to diabetes and hypoglycemia, cataract development, obesity, dental decay and arthritis. Sugar as well as corn gluten meal, wheat gluten meal, and rice gluten meal may be added to pet food to slow down the transition of rancid animal-fats. These glues and sweeteners hold the toxins in the food during digestion, causing the kidneys and the liver to work overtime ridding the body of these wastes. Noticeable allergic behavior to these substances are indicated when dogs chew their lower backs and lick their feet, which have become swollen.

•BALANCED DIETS.

Nutritional deficiencies can show up in your pet in many ways. The easiest to notice is dry, flaky skin and sparse, coarse, brittle hair coat. Becoming aware of what goes into your pet's food is the first step. Pet food companies have done a lot of research to make sure your animal receives the proper nutrients. We should thank them, and learn from them. Pet food manufacturers provide protein by including meat and certain vegetables, especially greens. If you decide to cook for your pet, you may leave out certain ingredients they need. Cats and dogs need different nutrients in different amounts than humans; therefore, human diets may not be suitable for Fido or Fluffy. Both dogs and cats need protein in their diets to provide specific animo-acids, which their bodies are unable to produce in sufficient quantity. Cats, for instance, are unable to manufacture taurine, therefore this must be provided by a meat-based diet. A taurine-deficient cat can develop feline central retinal degeneration, eventually leading to blindness, low weight, reduced growth, and also a fatal condition which weakens their heart muscle and causes death. Cats require eleven specific amino acids.

Dogs need ten amino acids in proper balance, as well as a high supply of methoinine and tryptophane. Although dogs tolerate vegetarianism better than cats, you still may be creating deficiencies that can lead to illness. Vegetarian diets must contain an excellent source of protein, such as wheat or barley grass, sea vegetables or nutritional yeast.

Animals need carbohydrates, which provide the body with energy. If a diet consists of an excessive amount of carbohydrates, the animal can develop diarrhea. Grains commonly used in pet food are wheat and soy. These are highly allergenic, and may make a dog chew at the root of his tail, and lick his feet. Amaranth and barley would be a better choice. Beet pulp is an excellent source of fiber for dogs, which paces the rate of digestion, and permits water to be properly removed from the colon. It also removes scale from collecting in the colon, is a source of vitamin B, and contains micronutrients.

White rice or Brewers' rice are commonly used fillers. They are devoid of nutrients, and should be avoided. All grains lose vitamins in storage, and many vitamins in meat may be destroyed in the canning process. To compensate, some manufacturers over-fortify their food with copious quantities of vitamins that most likely are not even assimilated by the body. This is because the enzymes needed for this process are destroyed when the food is cooked. Allergenic foods may ferment in the colon, sometimes for months, creating a very toxic environment. Not only does this create allergies, but it jeopardizes the health of the animal. Detoxifying is the only way to remove this debris, and switching to a premium "no-filler" food may be necessary to accomplish this task and maintain a healthy pet. We list a few stories that came to us regarding the need for giving premium foods.

→ *"In April, a Rottweiler breeder called me with her experience with a premium "health-food" dog food.[11] She said her dogs were switched from a "junk" food brand, and after a short while, some of the dogs lost weight, got bad breath and the urine and stools smelled awful. Some even expelled gas so foul, that the dogs had to be put outside. She had been using the food, and was almost ready to give up. Then one day when she was picking up the poop, she noticed pieces of yellow and black. Upon closer examination, she saw kernels of corn and fermenting black pieces of corn. She knew that the new food didn't contain corn. Then she remembered that eight months ago, in September, she had given the dogs some corn*

---

[11] Hund-N-Flocken by Solid Gold

cobs to chew on. For eight moths these kernels had been embedded inside the wall of the intestines, fermenting. This went on for a few days, then the stools firmed up and the smell went away. "
-as told to Solid Gold

→ "The vet said, 'there is just no hope. Just because your dog is urinating doesn't mean that he will make it. He is in the final stages of kidney failure; we can put him to sleep for you.' My reply was quick and right to the point; 'no thanks, I wouldn't do that to my dad and I won't do it to my dog either.'

That night as I drove the hour towards my home, Laddie laying weakly on the seat next to me, my thoughts flashed back over the last 13 years that I had been this dog's best friend. I remembered the years he lived with my dad, and the bond that the three of us shared together. I thought of the many miles that Laddie and I hiked through the wilderness, while I dealt with my grief and pain following the loss of my father. And now at 53, after taking a new lady, Laddie adjusted after a little jealousy. 'Well Laddie, this is probably our last trip together,' I said as I drove along towards home, fully expecting that he wouldn't make it through the next weekend. My lady had other ideas. She contacted a friend who had some pet products that maybe could help.

It was Monday night, and the dog didn't appear to be in any pain, so I had decided that if Laddie could hold on until the next Sunday, we could perhaps build a few more memories for a day or two. My lady's friend told us to get rid of the store-bought dog food, because it is just too hard on the kidneys; that was easy, because he hadn't eaten in a week. Next she advised us to give him an appetite stimulant,[12] and a wet mixture of vitamin C[13] along with a vitamin-mineral supplement[14]. We spoon fed Laddie, even though he was too weak to sit up, and soon he began drinking water into which we had put a Colloidal Silver supplement[15]. He then started licking a mixture of raw eggs, rice mixed with little chunks of chicken, and pork in gravy. By Sunday night any thoughts of "putting him down" were forgotten.

---

[12] DynaPro™, Dynamite® Specialty Products
[13] Dynamite Ester C®, Dynamite® Specialty Products
[14] Dynamite Showdown™, Dynamite® Specialty Products
[15] Solace™ Colloidal Silver, Dynamite® Specialty Products

Four months later, Laddie is back to his normal self, only now his diet is quite different. We are giving him a premium dog food,[16] and not too much, reducing his feeding to once a day in the evening. All I can say is this program worked for us, and obviously it works just fine for Laddie."
-Paul Tomblad, Redland, OR

Our dogs' and cats' diets also must consist of fats and oils which facilitate the transport and storage of fat-soluble vitamins. Some pet-food companies use sunflower, safflower and corn oils, high in Omega-6 essential fatty acids (EFA). Both dogs and cats need EFA's, for healthy metabolism, although the unbalancing of essential fatty acids (Omega-3 and Omega-6) can lead to disease. If oils high in Omega-6 are not balanced by Omega-3, found in flax, for example, they can cause tumor formations. Flax can stimulate the immune system and act as an antioxidant, as well as balance the effects of too large a quantity of Omega-6 oils. Fats, which provide EFA's, are carriers for fat-soluble vitamins, but may become rancid in stored meat or processed food. Rancid fat contributes to cancer and degenerative diseases such as heart problems and arthritis, according to the Surgeon General. Preservatives such as BHT and BHA are normally added to fight this problem, but a more natural choice would be vitamin C and E.

Manufacturers of the natural pet food products are diligent in preparing properly balanced meals and eliminating hazardous additives and by-products. It is prudent to trust their formulas. Their research has given them the tools to provide the nutrients each specific breed of animal needs. Supplementing pet diets with certain nutrients is advisable, but let the experts provide the basics. If you choose to cook for your pet, trust the advice of a professional such as this letter describes:

→ *"In general, until ten years ago, I had accepted the conventional western mode of "pet" rearing as the most beneficial. When our eight-week old Samoyed puppy, Tasha, joined our family, we gave her a diet of only grocery store puppy food. During that time, up until age five, Tasha had numerous attacks of cystitis and anal gland impactions. She had chronic bad breath, developed a fear of thunder and had attacks of hyperventilation. She has a heart murmur, and from the beginning, was diagnosed as*

---

[16] Dynamite® Premium Dog Food, Dynamite® Specialty Products

having congenital hip dysplasia. Her veterinarian in Minnesota said she wouldn't live very long, mainly because of her hip problems. Our determination to improve her quality of life kept us always looking for options.

We moved to the mountains of Wyoming, and here Tasha could take twenty-mile hikes, and run with the help of two complete hip replacements, but all of her other health problems worsened. Oozing sores began appearing on the outside and inside of Tasha's ears, and bald patches showed up on parts of her body. The sores could be eliminated with topical ointments, but they just kept reappearing. At that point I became desperate, but didn't know what to do for her. One day I picked up a copy of Dr. Pitcairn's 'Guide to Natural Health Care for Dogs & Cats. He described Tasha's symptoms perfectly, and I discovered that we had not been giving Tasha the best possible diet-regimen, as I had always thought! I followed Dr. Pitcairn's recommendation of detoxification, followed by a balanced fresh-food diet, vitamins, minerals and herbs.

She loved her new diet, and within a few weeks, her body began to respond positively. Our family was amazed! The oozing sores went away for good. Her hair grew back, and she had no more anal gland impactions, cystitis or bad breath. She kept her phobias, but we were able to strengthen her heart and reduce her arthritis with herbs."
-Estelle Hummel, Wyoming

Adequate nutrition is necessary for keeping our pet's teeth and gums healthy. While cavities represent the most common dental disease in humans, dogs and cats are more frequently prone to tartar buildup. This can lead to irritation of the gums, and ultimately cause inflammation and infection of the tooth and the root itself. Each animal accumulates tartar at a different rate, depending on its individual body chemistry. Generally, animals build up tartar faster as they age, than when they were young. Diet plays a part in this. Dry foods, since they are not as sticky as canned foods, do not adhere to the teeth as much, reducing the build up of tartar. Dry foods do not take tartar off, as some manufacturers lead us to believe. Rather, they act as tartar prevention.

Many people don't examine their pets' teeth often enough. They depend on visits to the vet for proper diagnosis of dental disease. You can be suspicious though, if your pet drools excessively, has bad breath, difficulty in eating, or has a change in temperament. Many pet owners have taken to brushing their pet's teeth. Believe me, this may be easy in a dog, but cats have a definite aversion to you sticking your fingers or a toothbrush in their mouths. Unfortunately, the only way to remove extreme tarter buildup is to let the vet handle the problem, usually resulting in anesthesia for the procedure. As long as your pet is healthy, and their immune system is strong, they should be able to handle the process without a problem. Dogs can be given bones or manufactured chews that are effective as tartar reducers. Cats do better if fed premium foods. Many "supermarket" varieties contain sugar and other ingredients that compromise the natural digestive juices in the mouth, and encourage food to remain on the teeth. Giving a cat an all-dry food diet may help reduce tartar, but the risk is that they can become dehydrated because of lack of moisture in the food. It is best to use a combination of both wet and dry, but make sure your cat drinks plenty of water after eating the dry food.

→ *"I saw an improvement in our nine-year old Akita when we changed to a premium dog food. However, our little dog, a stray that we had rescued, always had gum problems. Even after we had his teeth cleaned, his gums were always inflamed and tender, and he didn't like to chew on hard things. The vet said the gums were OK, but I felt he had some gum disease going on.*

I had to pulverize his vitamin to get him to eat it, so when I discovered a powdered supplement[17], it sounded good to me. We switched, and then I thought, why not try the food from the same manufacturer[18]. So we started him on it while we used our old food on our other dogs. Well, Roger's gums are now a normal color, although he still has a little dark pink line right at the base of the teeth. For the first time, his gums are looking pretty good. (I have also been brushing his teeth twice a week for a long time, and in the past I have given his gums a soaking with an herbal solution daily, so we had tried everything!) We feel this is a real breakthough, and it is due to the premium food and supplement. I am putting all my dogs on this food."
-Maggie Caplan, Sun City, AZ

---

[17] Dynamite Showdown®, Dynamite® Specialty Products
[18] Dynamite® Premium Dog Food, Dynamite® Specialty Products

• FAT CATS (AND DOGS)

Excess fat is no small problem for animals. In fact, obesity (15% higher than ideal body weight) is the most common form of malnutrition in dogs and cats. Pets are given too much food, and too little exercise. The junk foods found on supermarket shelves do not promote optimum weight. Dry kibble may taste good, but too much of it may turn Tabby into a fat cat. Dog treats given in excess could also lead your pet to obesity. Fat animals are predisposed to diabetes, certain forms of cancer and a shortened life. Trying to put your pet on a diet may tax your patience listening to their whines and dealing with personality changes not to mention the sad eyes that stare incessantly at you.

Photo by Bill Pratt

The new fad is "lite" pet foods, which means low fat. Some of these may actually have more calories than the regular brands. Soon to be in effect are new manufacturing requirements that detail specific caloric amounts for these diet foods. As we mentioned in Chapter 1, it is not the fats that contribute to obesity, but the type of fats. Do not be misled into purchasing low-fat foods as a "cure" for your pet's paunch.

One of the latest useful treatments for overweight animals is (-) Hydroxycitric acid (HCA), an herbal extract of the fruit Garcinia species (trees common to parts of South Asia). HCA is a close relative of the citric acid found in oranges, lemons and other citrus fruits. A major pharmaceutical company found that the extract of Garcinia acts within the cells to block the production of fat from carbohydrate calories. Even when laboratory animals were given diets that are 70% sugar, researchers found that HCA reduced food consumption, body fat and blood- lipid levels.

In Best Friends Animal Sanctuary in Utah, dogs fed maintenance diets supplemented with HCA and niacin-bound chromium showed an average weight loss of 8.6% below initial body weight, without calorie restriction, exercise or changes in feeding frequency over a five week period. HCA works by inhibiting the enzyme that changes carbohydrate calories to fats. Another ingredient that shows promise in aiding weight loss is chromium. Scientists have found that when bound to niacin, chromium will boost the action of insulin, improve the body's ability to burn fat, synthesize body protein and inhibit breakdown of muscle tissue.

Although applicability in animal nutrition has yet to be proven, chromium's beneficial effects have been shown in human studies.

Other fat-burning nutrients are being studied. L. Carnitine, inositol and choline, herbs such as guarana and Rhodiola rosea, and minerals could boost fat-burning in animals. Dietary substances that reduce appetite and body fat levels through natural physiological mechanisms could tilt the odds of reaching "ideal" weights in favor of success, and help dogs and cats enjoy the benefits of vitality and longevity with less risk of disease.

Dietary habit suggestions:
- Feed pets less and more often.
- Avoid junk-food brands of commercial pet foods.
- If food isn't eaten, remove it and offer it later.
- Give natural supplements. Pets are less likely to be hungry if their nutritional needs are satisfied.
- Don't give treats as rewards. Give love instead.
- Increase exercise (play with your animals)
- Provide plenty of pure water (to eliminate fats, waste, etc.)
- Watch for behavioral changes and (or) healing crises
- Monitor weight- loss and don't put your pet on a crash diet.
- Consult a veterinarian before starting any major weight-loss program for your pet.
- For underweight pets, don't go out and stock up on "bulk" foods such as cheap, dry kibble. This may compromise their nutrition. Instead, provide ample nutrients, high protein supplements, and minerals. By following many of the directions given in this book, you may find that if your pets are fed a normal quantity of premium food, they will fill out nicely.

Table scraps have gotten a bad rap as being a no-no for animal diets, yet most people are trained by their animals to share their dinners. If your animal is getting proper nutrition through natural canned or dry food, plus supplements, a few table scraps (organic, of course) won't hurt, depending on what you give them. Never feed cats or dogs pork, as it is high in preservatives, and carries a risk of trichinosis. Raw poultry should be avoided, to guard against bacteria infection. Turkey is OK, although its high amounts of tryptophan make lazy animals more lethargic. Tuna fish and cow's milk can trigger allergic reactions in cats and dogs, causing skin problems, hyperactivity, and asthma. The oil in tuna can rob your cat of vitamin E, resulting in a muscular disease called steatitis. If you give your cat tuna, supplement it with vitamin E.

Chocolate is a no-no for dogs and cats, as it contains theobromine, which can be fatal in quantity. Also, dogs cannot digest the whites of raw eggs, but cooked eggs are OK. Most veggies are a healthy snack. Beans can cause gas, unless supplemented with enzymes, and anyone who has been around a dog with gas will avoid beans. Most whole, unrefined grains are good for pets, if they want to eat them. Vary them, because any grain (especially wheat or corn) eaten on a regular or daily basis can create allergic reactions. This includes bread, cookies, chips, pasta, doggie cookies, etc. Refined grains and flours (white) should be avoided, as they have little nutritional value, and actually tax the body as it tries to digest them. Avoid treats with sugar, as this substance plays as much havoc on your pet's system as it does on your own. One woman discovered that a natural diet helped her pet so much that she developed healthy treats for him too:

→ *"Brunzi is my beautiful Golden Retriever. In October of 1992, I was devastated when I received a biopsy report on a lump that had been removed from Brunzi's face: squamous cell carcinoma; Prognosis: guarded. The thought that I may lose my little five-year-old "boy" was unbearable to me. I immediately took him to the vet, and he recommended a course of therapy that involved surgically removing all seven lumps that were on his body, implanting small metal disks at each incision and administering pinpoint radiation at all cancerous sites. (The reason for the metal disks was to precisely identify each site to radiate). This treatment would occur three times a week for seven weeks, and he would have to be anesthetized during each treatment.*

Needless to say, I was even more devastated after I left the hospital. I couldn't bear to subject him to the pain and horror for a treatment that did not guarantee his survival. I took him to a holistic veterinarian who addressed the cause of the lumps. What was causing Brunzi's immune system to function poorly? He put Brunzi on a variety of glandular, enzymatic, vitamin and mineral supplements based on his metabolic nutritional analysis. Brunzi underwent a two-week course of immunoaugmentative therapy, and I changed his diet. Whenever possible, I cooked fresh foods for him, using organically grown grains and free-range chickens. I used a super premium, dry dog food and continued his supplement program. For "snacks," I cooked my own organic dog cookies, which I started selling as Doggie Divines.

This regime worked! It has now been over three years since Brunzi's cancer diagnosis, and he's never been in better health. He now has a very important job. He is a therapy dog who visits his old-folk friends at a local nursing home several times a month."
-Carol Marangoni, New York

Supplementation is absolutely necessary for animals not fending for themselves in the wild. Cats require a higher concentration of vitamins and essential nutrients than any other animal in the world, including man! Mineral deficiencies, enzyme deficiencies, and essential fatty acid imbalance contribute to a compromised immune system in all species. An excellent indicator of nutritional deficiencies is the skin and coat of an animal. This includes disorders such as excessive shedding, hairballs in cats, bald patches, skin allergies, doggy odor, drippy eyes and hot spots.

In order for nutrients from food or vitamin supplementation to do their job in the body, they must be assimilated. By giving an animal vitamins that they can not break down (due to a lack of enzymes), you will just create a nutrient-rich litter box. Overcoming deficiencies in the basics of body chemistry will prevent this.

→ *"I am a hardened pet supplement skeptic. I own a twelve-year-old Scottish Terrier that has been on Prednisone injections and oral medication for eight years. I have seen innumerable veterinarians, tried special shampoos, powder supplements—more products and treatments than I could list. My dog Cinder has undergone complete allergy testing, which* reached the conclusion that this dog was allergic to nearly every natural and man-made product on the earth! Several vets concluded she must be immuno-deficient.

She had very little body hair, scratched incessantly, smelled awful and had frequent ear infections and staphylococus skin infections. My mother gave me a whole food concentrate supplement[19] and I tried it. I doubled the dosage for the first ninety days and continued giving it to Cinder for a year. I wish you could see my dog now. She has new hair growth, her scratching is greatly reduced and she has had only one ear infection in the past year. My vet is amazed! I changed nothing else in her diet, so now I am a believer in this supplement."
-Kaye Farrar, Missouri

→ "I love cats, and there was a litter of kittens born on my farm to a family of "barn" cats. As soon as they were weaned, I took one home and fed her regular cat food along with a flax-based supplement[20]. Although Pepper wasn't a "barn" cat anymore, she still traveled with me everyday to watch me work at the stables. She became noticeably bigger than her litter mates and never got any colds or runny eyes like the others. The only vet she ever saw was the barn vet who gave her a rabies shot.

When she was about two years old, I decided to adopt another "barn" kitten. Before I took him home, I thought it wise to have him tested for feline leukemia because some of the "barn" cats all of a sudden started dying from this disease. Ironically, the new kitten was negative and my Pepper was positive! I had her tested three more times with identical results. She showed no ill effects and still played like a kitten, but alas, she was positive and my vet told me that she was probably born that way. Pepper Puss is now eleven years old, still has a beautiful thick, soft, slate gray coat, and continues to amaze the vets and me that she is still alive and active. I can only attest to the fact that because I'm giving her the live enzymes and amino acids that are found in the supplement, she is alive and thriving."
-Janis Gianforte, New Jersey

---

[19] Missing Link, whole food supplement by Designing Health, Inc..
[20] NUPRO, by Nutri-Pet Research

This book is about preventive measures you can take to keep your pet in tip-top shape. In this chapter, we will describe some of the common 'home' remedies that you can investigate. We still advise that you receive a proper diagnosis and recommendation from an allopathic or holistic veterinarian before proceeding with any natural medications.

•HERBS.

Herbs have been used for centuries for healing and illness prevention. Domestic and wild animals still go to plants naturally when they need medication or internal cleansing. Herbs are natural sources of vitamins, antioxidants, minerals, enzymes, amino acids, proteins, sugars, carbohydrates, chlorophyll, trace elements and essential fatty acids. They are balanced, and therefore easily assimilated by the body. Herbs work in partnership with the body and help the body to heal itself. Herbs assist in the healing process by helping the body to eliminate toxins, thus reducing symptoms. They may stimulate physiological processes like emptying of the bowels or bladder, or act as a liver cleanse, and can serve as immune-system builders. Success with herbs can be seen through the following stories:

→ *"I am Pervis the Cat, and I'm five years old. When I was one-and-a-half years old, the vet told my owner, Mike, I'd come down with feline infectious peritonitis (FIP). I had constant diarrhea and vomiting, and was down to four pounds. The vet suggested I be put to sleep. (I thought I was too young to die!)*

My owner thought there must be an answer, so he tried 5cc of liquid aged garlic extract[21] every two hours, five times a day. In four weeks, I'd gained my weight back, and was playing with the other cats. Best of all, none of my friends contracted FIP. After six weeks, Mike took me back to the vet, and was he amazed. He had never seen or heard of any cat that had survived FIP. I'm happy to say I'm still in perfect health."
-Pervis the Cat, California

Chinese herbs are normally *custom-tailored* to the individual needs of the patient. Chinese herbs have to be adapted to each condition for pets, in regards to dosage and liver function. If an animal's disharmony is too hot, they use cooling herbs; too cool, heating herbs. If there is pain or "stagnation of Qi" (the energy or life force that circulates through a body),

---

[21] Kyolic® Aged Garlic Extract™ by Wakunaga of America Co., Ltd.

they seek herbs that disperse that stagnation, thereby alleviating the pain. Since they are not able to get exact information from the animals on how they feel, they carefully supervise and observe the patient, and monitor the effects of the herbs administered, to assure success. There are little or no side effects when a balanced formula is administered. Chinese herbs are effective for chronic conditions such as arthritis, and undefinable conditions like anxiety. They are normally not effective for acute conditions needing immediate treatment, such as shock.

→ *"Mishu, a cat, had a history of urinary crystals, that always resulted in pain, bleeding and an eventual trip to the vet to resolve the problem. Not only was the owner uncomfortable because of the vet bill, but poor Mishu was constantly in pain. His owner changed Mishu's diet as was prescribed by the vet, but his condition only improved while using an herbal formula containing herbs that break down the stones and help wash out the fine sandy gravel that is found in the urinary tract.[22] It is a cooling formula that promotes the flow of water so the 'heat' of the infection and stones are balanced and dispersed. Since using this formula, Mishu has been free of urinary tract crystals for over three years, with no adverse effects."*
-Laura Mignosa, Connecticut

"Western" herbology is more available over-the-counter, and familiarization with each plant's healing properties is essential. Any herb used as a medicinal, should be recommended by a skilled herbal practitioner, to avoid harmful dosages or inaccurate diagnosis. Some herbs are great for dogs, but not healthy for cats. For instance, Willowbark is known to be toxic to felines. Herbal formulas have been known to successfully treat arthritis, hip dysplasia, skin problems, hair loss, vomiting, respiratory infections, bladder and kidney disorders, and a host of other maladies. As a reference, we will list some common herbs that you may consider using. As with any illness, we recommend that you consult a veterinarian or alternative practitioner.

---

[22] Crystal Clear, from Herb-Cetera

The following report from Aequus Veterinary Service outlines treatment with herbs.

→ *CASE 3: 13 year old Standard **Poodle**.*

Complaint: Weight loss, slight ataxia in hindquarters, lethargy, sudden aged appearance, and possible mental deterioration (delayed response to stimuli, confusion with doors and corners of rooms).

Exam: Dog was fairly bright and alert, but there appeared to be hearing loss, as the dog did not seem to respond to low frequency voices or calls. The dog was approximately five to ten percent below ideal body weight. Mild ataxia was present in hind legs with marked wear of dorsal surface of hind nail. There was moderate atrophy of both hamstring muscle groups. Mental attitude was one of anxiety and timidity.

Treatment: The dog was chiropractically adjusted. Dietary recommendations were made to remove the dog from processed dry food and be put on partially cooked meatloaf diets (Pitcairn). Pastas, grains and vegetables were recommended as often as the dog would eat, until weight was closer to ideal. Dog was put on Bach Rescue Remedy and Vetri-Science Cell-Advance 880.

Response: Two months post treatment, dog is continuing to show improvement, both physically and mentally. She is no longer acting as timid and subordinate around other dogs and strangers. The owner thinks she can hear better. Appetite has improved, and dog is gaining weight. Dog has had Vetri-Science Vetri-Disk, Vetri-Science GlycoFlex 600 and Coyote Springs, Senior Support combination herbs added to the above regimen.

Following is a partial list of herbs for pets, along with some of their benefits. For a more comprehensive look at herbal healing methods for animals, read *The Natural Remedy Book for Dogs & Cats* by Diane Stein, *Your Cat Naturally* by Grace McHattie, or the chapter "Alternative Healing Options For Pets" in Linda Rector Page's book, *Healthy Healing*. Again, please consult your holistic veterinarian prior to administering herbs, as some may be toxic to specific animal species.

•**Alfalfa** contains every vitamin and mineral. It acts as a blood cleanser and detoxifier, and is used for allergies, arthritis, kidney and urinary infections and as a tonic.

•**Aloe Vera** is an excellent colon cleanser and remedy for soothing the stomach, liver, kidneys, spleen and bladder. It contains anti-inflammatory agents, and has been called the 'wound hormone." It has the ability to penetrate all seven layers of the skin, for maximum healing.

•**Arnica** in herbal tincture or cream form, is useful in pain reduction of sprains and bruises. Can affect sensitive skin if used undiluted.

•**Barberry** is mainly used in the treatment of liver problems. It promotes the flow of bile, stimulates digestion and appetite, and lessens constipation.

•**Bearberry** soothes and tones the lining of the bladder and helps the urinary tract. It is antiseptic and diuretic and helpful for cystitis, bladder stones, incontinence and kidney failure.

•**Black Walnut** is excellent to treat skin conditions. It is useful to expel internal parasites and tapeworms.

•**Boswella** is a potent herb for inflammatory disease such as arthritis. This gummy extract from the Boswella tree is being used on horses and dogs with great success. It acts by mechanism similar to non-steroidal groups of anti-arthritic drugs, with a plus being very few side effects.

•**Buchu** helps in the treatment of cystitis and bladder weakness.

•**Burdock** is useful in treating dry skin, scalp, hair and for eczema. It also has been helpful with rheumatism. Burdock root is alkalizing and soothing to the stomach and intestines.

•**Calendula**, or marigold, is used on the skin for fast healing of wounds. It reduces swelling, and is regenerating as well as anti-microbial. Caution: Calendula closes the skin rapidly so in the case of abscesses, make sure the wound has drained completely before applying.

•**Cascara Sagrada** is nature's answer to a laxative.

•**Catnip,** in addition to being an aphrodisiac for cats, can help with fever, flatulence and digestive pain, soothe nerves and act as a sedative.

•**Cat's Claw (Una de Gato)** active constituents, oindole alkaloids, have been proven to increase the ability of the white blood cells and macrophages to attack and digest abnormal cells, harmful microorganisms and toxic matter. The inner bark contains the medicinal properties. Results with humans include help for tumors, arthritis, allergies, respiratory infections, parasites, and intestinal disorders. Similar success can be expected in animals as well. Cat's Claw contains numerous plant substances that have tremendous antioxidant properties more powerful than vitamin E and C. Although this herb is considered non-toxic, recommended dosages for animals should not exceed 50-100 mg. per ten pounds of body weight, without consulting a practitioner.

•**Cayenne pepper,** or Capsicum, is described as a blood stimulant as well as an insect repellent, if taken internally. It also is useful in treating worms, as an antiseptic, and can improve appetite and ease colic. It has been used to help stop shock and aid in heart seizure.

•**Chamomile** is an antispasmodic, and also a sedative. It works to reduce stomach pains, colic and earache. Topically, it can draw out skin toxins and help with inflammations. An extract of this herb is commonly used in moisturizers, due to the high content of levomenol (an anti-inflammatory agent that is excellent at soothing dry and cracked skin.)

•**Comfrey** is a natural soother, internally and externally. It aids in healing of burns, skin ulcers, cuts, abscesses, insect bites, bruises, boils, sprains, fractures and swelling. Comfrey causes bacteria to multiply so rapidly that it implodes upon itself, due to weak cell walls, and then disintegrates, making it an excellent treatment against bacteria.

•**Couchgrass** leaves are eaten by dogs and cats to induce vomiting, or as a laxative. Birds eat the seeds for bladder ailments and constipation. The silica content of Couchgrass helps to strengthen teeth, beaks and claws.

•**Dandelion** is useful in treating liver problems. It has a powerful diuretic effect, and because of its cleansing nature, can help arthritis and rheumatism. Its bitter taste helps promote digestion and appetite.

•**Dill** improves appetite and digestion, and is food for relief of flatulence.

•**Echinacea** is nature's antibiotic, and should be used *medicinally*, not on a regular basis. This extract can be painted on ringworm to dry it up. When mixed with Black Walnut extract diluted, can expel worms such as pinworms and tapeworms.

•**Elderberry** is used in the treatment of bruises and sprains. It also works for constipation and catarrhal inflammation of the upper respiratory tract. If taken over a period of time, will help purify the blood.

•**Eucalyptus** is well known for its antiseptic action, and for its use in treating respiratory conditions. Historically, as an inhalant, it has been used to treat influenza in horses and distemper in dogs.

•**Garlic** is known as the supreme immunizer antioxidant and helps in preventing fleas, worms, ticks, lice, gastric and skin problems. Animals in the wild periodically seek out areas of garlic. This herb is of value in treating fevers, skin conditions, respiratory tract problems, some gastrointestinal conditions, rheumatism, and as a general antiseptic and cleanser. It also helps to restore the gut flora following disturbances, and helps the heart by lowering blood pressure.

•**Ginger** is a stimulant, and can ease stomach and bowel pains. It is good assisting in decongesting nasal passages.

•**Goldenseal** is also an antibiotic, a sulfa equivalent. It can be used with echinacea to dry up ringworm, but it will stain fur.

•**Hawthorn** is one of the best herbs for the heart and for circulation. It also is useful as a heartworm preventive.

•**Horsetail** is a rich source of silica, needed to keep the skin moist and elastic. This herb is good to repair scar tissue, and eliminate swelling. It imparts strength to nails and luster to the skin and coat.

•**Juniper** is a diuretic, and is used in cases of cystitis and urethritis.

•**Licorice** is a good expectorant, and is used for treating bronchitis and respiratory problems, coughs, catarrhal conditions, and even chronic constipation and skin conditions. Because of licorice's glycyrrhizin content, it is a good alternative for steroid therapy, used to relieve inflammation without drug side-effects. Glycyrrhizin stimulates the adrenals into action, while introducing its own anti-inflammatory, antimicrobial, immune-supporting corticosteroid-like reaction to the body.

•**Milk Thistle** has been use for centuries as folk remedies for boils and skin diseases, hepatitis and liver problems, especially those associated with environmental pollution. Since the liver takes the most abuse from the toxic lifestyles we inflict on our pets, the preservative and chemical-laden food we give them, and the drugs and chemical flea collars, sprays, to shampoos we subject them, they need something to help detoxify their bodies. Milk thistle can assist in the cleansing of these pollutants from their bodies.

•**Mullein** helps relieves congestion.

•**Neem** seeds and leaves have been used to construct a new class of "soft" insecticides that are non-toxic to animals, birds and even beneficial insects. It does not affect the nervous system and is non-toxic if ingested. Topically, it is useful against fungi, allergies and mange, ringworm, eczema, infections and internal parasites. It can protect pets from fleas, ticks and mites without harming the animal. It is also useful as a garden and lawn spay in place of toxic chemicals, which will affect pets who play outdoors.

•**Nettles** are known to help rheumatism, arthritis and skin disorders. Also, because of its diuretic effect, it helps cleanse the blood and is indicated in bladder and urinary infections. Historically, it has been used as a tonic for the coat, making the hair shine, removing scurf and as a valuable treatment for eczema. Some suggest using it as a treatment for anemia, because of its high iron content.

•**Parsley** is a rich source of vitamins B, C, A, potassium and iron, thereby being a good blood- strengthener. It also helps with joint stiffness, bad breath, obesity and bladder problems. It can reduce flatulence and increase milk production in nursing bitches.

•**Pau D'arco** provides resistance to various infections as it possesses antibiotic properties.

•**Peppermint** promotes digestion by smoothing muscle tissue of the stomach, and eases gas pains. It also can help with motion sickness, and is known to restore appetites in dogs .

•**Raspberry Leaf** assists whelping by strengthening the pelvic muscles, toning the uterus and reducing the risk of hemorrhage. It helps to bring fluid to the birth canal to help prevent dry painful births.

•**Skullcap** has a reputation as a general tonic for the nervous system. It has long been used in the treatment of epilepsy and rabies. It has a calming effect, and is useful in cases of excitability, nervous spasms, fits and paralysis.

•**Slippery elm** is good for very young, old or weak cats and dogs. It coats inflamed tissue internally and is useful for ulcers, constipation, diarrhea, dysentery and colitis. Externally it can be used on wounds, burns, abscesses, and insect bites.

•**Southernwood** is a de-wormer for dogs and cats. It also acts as a heartworm preventive for dogs, given every other day from April to October. It makes blood bitter in animals, and they become less appealing to mosquitoes.

- **Valerian** works as a sedative, and as a calming herb for nervousness and excitability. It acts on the higher nerve centers, promoting sleep and in some situations, reducing pain.
- **Yarrow** stops internal bleeding, and is good for fevers. It may be helpful for diabetic animals, as its chemical makeup is close to insulin. Externally, yarrow is an antiseptic for rashes, wounds, and deep punctures.
- **Yew** is a medicinal herb currently harvested from the bough tips of the Yew tree. It is effective for bursitis, joint problems, arthritis, skin problems such as allergy rashes, big bites, basal-cell carcinoma skin cancer. Historically, Native Americans have used the yew for pain, fever, colds, stomach distress, as a diuretic and to alleviate the pain during the birthing process.
- **Yucca** is useful as a laxative, diuretic and antiseptic. It is helpful for ulcers, sore joints and arthritis, and as a pain reliever and an effective anti-viral and anti-fungal agent.
- **Velvet Antler**—although this is not an herb, it works similarly to herbs in the healing process. Harvested humanely from deer and elk, the antler velvet has shown to have the ability to repair joint injuries and reduce inflammation from arthritis. It has also been reported useful in preventing bladder and kidney stones.

We have had many reports of extraordinary success with using herbs for both healing (such as garlic) and illness prevention (echinacea). These stories provide first hand information on the benefits of herbs:

→ *"We have several cats, and have recently had a problem with Murray, our two year old. He came home one day with a hole in his leg. It was incredibly raw. I could easily tell that he was in tremendous pain. The hole was so large that we were sure we would have to take him to the vet for stitches. The only thing that came to mind was that someone must have shot my Murray! My husband had recently purchased a pet spray[23], that included minerals, chamomile, comfrey, burdock root, horsetail and aloe vera. We decided to try this on Murray, and were amazed that he sat there during the application (cats usually panic when sprays are used). We sprayed it on the raw area several times a day. By the next morning, I was shocked to see how much improvement had occurred. After a few days, the wound was only a shadow of what it had once been. About a month later, my ten-year old son David, cut himself, and I used the skin spray on him. Within an hour, his injury had already begun to scab over."*
-Theresa Aponte, Florida

---

[23] Skin-Lyte™, by Nature's Path.

→ *"When I moved from Arizona to California, my calico cat, Amber, had to adjust from being an outdoor cat to living in a small apartment. Needless to say, having her freedom curtailed was a shock for her, and she didn't handle it so well. Amber stopped bathing herself regularly, and her coat became greasy and wouldn't lay flat. Normally, she was a very affectionate cat, but after the move she became whiny and mean. The straw that broke the camel's back was when she started to use the shower as a litter box. My husband gave me an ultimatum that was getting to the point of the marriage or the cat.*

I asked a vet for some advice and they told me she was stressed out and I should find a way to calm her down. I tried various things, but the one that worked was a liquid garlic extract[24] squirted onto a saucer that she lapped up. Within a few days, her appetite improved markedly, followed by her disposition. She went back to using the litter box, and she started bathing herself again. Soon she was calm enough that I could hold her again and I noticed that her fur was softer than ever. My husband gave her a reprieve. Little did I know that liquid garlic extract could help relieve stress in an animal. It sure helped to save our marriage."
-Karen Melville, California

→ *"I adopted a rescued adult greyhound a couple of years ago. Though his teeth were mostly in good shape, he had bad breath due to the plaque caked on his molars. Rather than risk stressing out poor Reno, by going to the vet and having his teeth scraped, I searched for an all-natural product. I saw an advertisement for a natural dental bone[25] with wheat germ and chlorophyll, which I purchased and gave to Reno. He loved the bone and now has no plaque left on his teeth. I am very impressed with this healthy and less traumatic way to clean my dog's teeth."*
-Karen Peiper, Venice, Florida

→ *"As a naturopathic consultant, I am always interested in products that will be beneficial to my clients, human and animal. Our three geriatric Papillons all have some signs of arthritic development, especially on damp days. I had started them on a homeopathic tincture of "devil's claw", which is an anti-inflammatory. The response to the treatment was good. I received a sample of Super Oxy Green[26] and gave the 16 lb. dog ½*

---

[24] Kyolic® Aged Garlic Extract™ by Wakunaga of America Co., Ltd.
[25] Greenies from Pet Central, Inc.
[26] Super Oxy Green, Pet Central, Inc.

tablet daily, and the other two 6 lb. dogs, ¼ tab. The response at the end of the week was phenomenal. All three dogs have acquired a new breath of life as they run up and down the stairs, play outside, and chase balls. They act like young puppies. We have recommended this supplement to other pet owners."
-Louis E. Rousseau, M.T. BLD, Naturopathic Consultant, Dracut, MA

•FLOWER REMEDIES

In the 1930's, the noted British physician, Dr. Edward Bach developed the natural healing methods of flower remedies. He believed that reducing stress, and emotional imbalances were important in creating a healthy body. Flower remedies address every emotional condition and imbalance that can contribute to illness. They address the cause of the problem, not the symptom, and are all natural, and safe. These remedies work by addressing emotions only, and do not interfere with any other type of treatment or with any physical functioning. Among the many emotions that flower remedies can help are sadness, rage, nervousness and stress from travel in carriers and crates, on airplanes, cars and trains.

Flower remedies normally come in liquid form and can be given to your pet diluted in water. Although normally preserved in alcohol, many tinctures use minimal amounts that do not seem to affect pets.

photo by Neil Shively

We have used flower remedies and have found them to be extremely effective for lessening the shyness in cats, and for reducing aggressive behavior found by some animals in multi-pet households. The following story comes from success by a breeder.

→ *"I have been showing cats for many years, and recently noticed that my cats appeared much more fidgety than many of the other cats being shown. It began to concern me, so I spoke to several of the other exhibitors, who suggested that I use a five-flower remedy.[27] It was fantastic. For the first time, my prize show-cat sat calmly before, and during the show.*

---

[27] Deva Flower Remedies by Natural Labs.

She was rewarded with a ribbon at the show. Since then, I have used it with my cats before we leave for the show, when we arrive, and about ten minutes before showing. We've had our best results ever!"
-M.G., New Mexico

Following is a list of flower remedies and the emotional conditions they help:

Flower Remedies

•**Aspen** is used for calming nerves on animals that are easily frightened, especially of the unknown.
•**Cherry Plum** is useful on aggressive animals that appear uncontrollable.
•**Chestnut Bud** targets animals that are difficult to train. It helps correct unhealthy habits and negative behavior.
•**Chicory** can be for an animal that follows you around, is constantly underfoot and becomes extremely upset when left alone. For the jealous pet.
•**Clematis** can be used on lethargic pets.
•**Impatiens** can be used on impatient, fast-paced, irritable animals.
•**Larch** is effective in helping animals that lack self-confidence in the pecking order.
•**Mimulus** is for reducing fears of timid animals.
•**Rock Rose** helps animals that panic easily or who have experienced terror.
•**Scleranthus** alleviates car-sickness.
•**Star of Bethlehem** works on animals who have been abused or who have lost a loved pet or human companion.
•**Water Violet** is for the animals who tend to be loners (especially cats).
•**Five Flower Remedies** include a wide-range of flower essences that are used for trauma. They can also be used as a calming agent for travel, after surgery or accidents, for panicked animals, or anytime stress reduction is needed. They normally include Star of Bethlehem, Rock Rose, Clematis, Cherry Plum and Impatiens.

•HOMEOPATHIC TREATMENTS

Homeopathic treatments, available for over two-hundred years, are becoming more mainstream, and people now are considering their usage for pets. Basically, homeopathy treats an illness by the stimulation of the body's own healing process, much like a vaccination, only without much risk for a reaction. These remedies are prepared from natural plant substances. They are delivered in micro-doses, thereby highly reducing the risk of side-effects or toxicity.

Since homeopathy views the individual as a whole, symptoms and signs from the body, mind and spirit are all taken into consideration when selecting treatment. For example, if you peel an onion, your eyes burn, your nose runs or you begin to sneeze. If those same symptoms appear when you get a cold, a minute dose of homeopathic Allium cepa (the red onion) would help your body heal itself. There are more than 100 double blind clinical studies which document the efficacy of homeopathic remedies. Dosages are available in tablets, liquids, suppositories and ointments. The most popular form is pellets, taken sublingually (under the tongue). These pellets dissolve quickly, are easy to administer to pets.

When you see a homeopathic remedy, the dilution will be indicated on the label. X-potencies are diluted by using one part of the mother tincture, and nine parts alcohol or water. As we continue the series of dilutions, we obtain 2X 3X, etc. C-potencies are diluted by using one part of the mother tincture and ninety-nine parts of alcohol or water, therefore 2C, 3C, etc. Different individual indications require different potencies.

Homeopathic medicines need some special consideration. Storage of containers is important. They should be kept away from light and sources of electrical appliances, as these can diminish the potency. Do not feed your animal for fifteen minutes either before or after giving the remedy, and don't give your dog chocolate (not good for them anyway), as this negates the effect. Make sure your pet is off drugs such as antibiotics, antihistamines, anti-inflammatories and anesthetic agents as they can possibly interfere with homeopathic action. These remedies should not be used, unless they have been prescribed by a practitioner familiar with the animal. If you get a reaction to a remedy, you may antidote it with coffee or another homeopathic remedy recommended by your homeopath. A few stories that were sent to us reveal the use of homeopathic medicine for skin ailments.

→ *"My five-year-old Golden Retriever developed a terrible skin condition, due to allergies. She lost all her hair on her hind end, tail and legs, and scratched her face raw until it was bloody. I felt so sorry for her, yet I didn't want to resort to antibiotics and steroids. I sought counsel with a homeopathic vet who treated her with acupuncture and nutritional therapy. The first two weeks I didn't see an improvement. Then I purchased a bottle of Newton Labs Homeopathic Skin Drops and gave it to my dog. Her itching began to subside, her skin became healthy and her hair full-bodied again within a few months. She looked younger and more vibrant!"*
-Marie Dizon, California

→ *"I took in a stray female cat whose fur was in terrible shape. She was really allergic to fleas. I have looked for over two years for flea products that were not commercial poisons, to help my cat friends. At first, Betty's coat was in such bad shape that she had to have cortisone shots. Then I started using a homeopathic remedy in her daily drinking water[28]. Two weeks later, I noticed a remarkable improvement in her coat. Hair that broke off two inches above the tail started growing back, and her really thin coat along her backbone also started to thicken. She now has a lush winter coat and is so much more comfortable. She has fewer fleas, since I have also used a homeopathic remedy for flea relief."*
-Merilea, California

Some of the more common homeopathic remedies are listed below.

Homeopathic Remedies

- **Allium cepa** (Red onion) for colds, flu, violent sneezing, sore throat.
- **Arnica montana** (Mountain daisy) for bruises, traumas, injuries, muscular tiredness and pain.
- **Belladonna** (Deadly nightshade) for fever, colds, flu.
- **Calcarea fluorica** (Calcium fluoride) for joint pain, cysts, lumbago.
- **Calcarea sulphurica** (Calcium sulphate) for burns, boils, eczema.
- **Ferrum phosphoricum** (Iron phosphate) for colds, low fever and congestion, cough.
- **Kali muriaticum** (Potassium chloride) for ear, nose and throat catarrhal inflammations, runny nose, sore throat, mouth ulcers, dandruff.
- **Kali phosphoricum** (Potassium phosphate) for convalescence following flu or infectious disease, or exhaustion from nervousness.
- **Kali sulphuricum** (Potassium sulphate) for colds, yellow nasal discharge, scaly skin eruptions.
- **Natrum muriaticum** (Sodium chloride) for eczema, tendency to catch cold, fright, dandruff.
- **Natrum phosphoricum** (Sodium phosphate) for flatulence, indigestion, belching, vomiting, rheumatism of the knee joint, itching skin.
- **Nux vomica** (Poison nut) for upset stomach, constipation.
- **Pulsatilla** (Wind flower) for nasal congestion, chronic irritation of mucous membranes.
- **Rhus toxicodendron** (Poison Ivy) for rheumatic pain, muscle pain, sprains, flu-like symptoms, poison ivy.
- **Staphysagria** (Stavesacre) for urinary complaints with burning pain on urination, hypersensitivity of genitals, eczema of the scalp or face.
- **Sulphur** (Brimstone) for itchy or burning skin eruptions, rashes, eczema, diarrhea, recurring sties.

---

[28] Homepathic remedies for pets by Dr. Goodpet.

•VITAMINS AND OTHER NUTRIENTS

Pets need minerals, essential fatty acids and enzymes, and other nutrient supplementation. Steven Hartmann of Green Foods Corporation said during an interview by Dr. Anthony J. Cichoke (Health Food Business, July 1995), "despite manufacturer claims to the contrary, modern processing methods used in the pet food industry can destroy the vital vitamins necessary to maintain optimum health as well as live enzymes that animals require for proper digestion." Vitamins and minerals provided by ingredients in commercial pet food are often variable. Grains lose vitamins in storage, and niacin (B3) and Thiamine (B1) found in meat are destroyed during the canning process. Dry foods are made with an extruder, grinding the mixture together, adding water and steam, cooking at high temperatures and then having fat or animal tissue coatings that have been chemically or enzymatically predigested, applied to enhance the palatability. Vitamins must now be added back, and although the manufacturers try hard, the level of the various vitamins, especially the antioxidants, might not be sufficient to maintain optimal health.

Animals, like humans, need to add supplements to their diets for optimum nutrition. Probiotics, vitamins, nutritional yeast and garlic, greens, along with other nutrient supplements all have their place in balancing the body for maintaining health and curing ills. In most cases, supplementation is definitely beneficial to your pet. Dogs and cats vary in nutritional requirements, so vitamin and mineral supplements are formulated with those differences in mind. For instance, cats require a higher concentration of vitamins and essential nutrients than any other animal. They need a good supply of calcium and phosphorus in balanced amounts. Cats (unlike dogs) do not have the ability to convert beta carotene to vitamin A; therefore, they require preformed vitamin A.

Vitamin C is normally manufactured by the animals' body, if given the proper balance of nutrients; but during times of stress or illness, supplementation may be necessary. Dogs with joint disorders, stiffness and arthritic conditions have been shown to improve significantly during clinical trials where calcium ascorbate was administered. This vitamin is also useful in cats to protect them against a common ailment, cystitis (urinary gravel).

When animals forage, they include greens in their diet. Domestic cats and dogs may nibble on nothing more than grass, but this gives us an indication of their need for chlorophyll, known as concentrated sun power. Chlorophyll is to the plant as blood is to the animal. It is a natural blood builder, and also heals wounds by stimulating repair of damaged tissues, and inhibiting growth of bacteria. It has been known to cure acute infections of the respiratory tract, and controls halitosis. As an antioxidant, it even has shown to nullify the effects of environmental and food pollutants. It can actually be more effective than vitamin C, E, or A, and be an effective preventive measure for cancer. Chlorophyll is found in greens, especially when the plant is young, before it begins to grow branches.

Chlorophyll is also abundant in cereal grasses such as wheat and barley. These are easily obtainable in supplement form, and contain high amounts of protein. Grasses are rich in magnesium, considered to be an excellent blood and kidney cleanser and blood cooler in hot weather, rich in antioxidants and due to their high enzyme content, wheat and barley grass are powerful detoxifiers. Many vegetables contain incomplete proteins, and can't be totally utilized by the body. Wheat and barley grasses contain all twenty amino acids and therefore are a bioavailable source of protein.

Sea vegetables, algae and Chlorella are also an excellent source of not only chlorophyll, but minerals and vitamin C. Kelp is high in minerals, especially calcium, iodine, potassium, and magnesium, and is a good source of vitamin C. It is effective against respiratory infections, and intestinal and urinary problems. Its iodine content aids digestion, and increases assimilation of fatty elements in food. Kelp causes better retention and utilization of calcium and phosphorus, contributing to shiny coat and skin health. Chlorella is a single-cell algae It is rich is chlorophyll, minerals, vitamin A, B2, B3, B6, and high in protein and vitamin C. It has been an effective treatment for ulcers, cancer, colds and vicious bacteria, as well as an excellent immune booster. Blue green algae and spirulina are also excellent sources of proteins, vitamins and minerals. Since your pets can't ask for greens, you may want to consider adding one of the powdered or pill supplements to their diet. Seaweeds are the most concentrated natural source of broad-spectrum micronutrients left on earth. The mature plants are composed of more than 60 minerals and trace elements (naturally chelated by the plant), and a broad array of vitamins, amino acids, antioxidants, essential fatty acids and phytochemicals.

Humanely harvested from deer and elk, antler velvet has been used for centuries as an aphrodisiac. Most recently, its healing properties have been discovered. Notable for pets is its anti-inflammatory properties, which facilitate rapid tissue repair after injury. Containing glucosamine and chondroitin sulfate, it helps rebuild cartilage and improves joint mobility in pets suffering from arthritis. It is useful in cases of anemia, and helps stimulate the formation of red blood cells. Antler velvet improves liver function and strengthens the immune system.

Garlic, an herb, has been an all around remedy for hundreds of years. We single it out because it is effective against bacteria, viruses, funguses and parasites. It has also been tested as a treatment for cancer, where it was found that aged garlic extract was more effective than raw garlic. Aged garlic extract has the allicin (the smelly part) removed. Allicin was once thought to be the most effective part of garlic. New studies confirm that is not the case, whereby allicin can actually be toxic, and kill cells. Aged garlic extract is a more effective form of this superb antioxidant herb. Animals are treated with garlic for fevers, pulmonary, gastric and skin conditions, rheumatism, parasitic infestation, worms, ticks, lice. When taken with nutritional yeast, garlic can be an effective flea repellent, as the skin takes on an odor that the fleas don't like. Garlic is an anti-bacterial, and therefore is useful for abscesses, and to prevent infection from open wounds. This story makes a good point for taking your time in choosing a course of treatment for your pet illnesses (unless they are critical). It is also good to get a second opinion on radical procedures.

Below are listed some of the more common natural remedies.

Natural remedies

•**Alfalfa** is considered highly nourishing, in addition to being a rich source of trace minerals. It is high in chlorophyll, which can have a cleansing action on the body, detoxifying and preventing odors.

•**Aloe Vera** has remarkable healing powers both internally and externally as a cleanser, detoxifier and normalizer. It can penetrate all seven layers of the skin, permeating to the germinal layer carrying nutrients, is rich in mucopolysaccharides (pulls water out of the air to moisten skin), and contains anti-inflammatory agents. It is used for treatment of wounds, scar prevention, eczema, burns, rashes, swellings, abrasions, irritation and itching.

•**Antioxidants** such as vitamins C, E, A, fight infection and disarms free radicals. They may help prevent cataracts. Vitamin C helps promote healing, is an immune strengthener, and helps reduce arthritis pain. It works best when taken with vitamin E, one of nature's powerful antioxidants. Vitamin E is added to pet food to retard spoilage. Vitamin E is found in the oil of the wheat germ, corn, sunflower and cottonseed, egg yolks and liver.

•**Bee pollen** is rich in nutrients and live enzymes Pollen is a potent source of RNA and DNA. It also contains abundant quantities of rutin, which strengthens capillaries, is a blood builder, and strengthens fertility in breeding, as well as combating allergies. It may control the runaway growth of cancer cells because of its antioxidant vitamins A and E. High in lecithin, bee pollen helps increase brain functions, a plus for senior animals. It is richer in amino acids than any animal source, containing five to seven times more amino acids than beef, eggs and cheese of equal weight. This is significant, because the protein quality in most commercial pet foods is very low. Because of its vast range of nutrients, bee pollen is extremely beneficial for the immune system.

•**Biotin** is a B-vitamin that is thought to act as a coenzyme, and is necessary for certain reactions incorporating amino acids into protein, as well as being essential for thyroid, adrenal and nervous-system health. Biotin deficiencies in dogs and cats can appear as skin disorders, loss of hair, and eczema, as well as weak hindquarters and stiffness. Sometimes these deficiencies are misdiagnosed as dermatitis or flea bites, and drugs are administered as a "cure" which can further aggravate the biotin loss. Biotin loss can be provoked by the animals eating raw egg whites, which contain avidin (the protein that interferes with biotin absorption). Cooking the egg will destroy the avidin, therefore if you give your animals eggs, make sure they are cooked.

•**Boswella** is a potent herb for inflammatory disease such as arthritis. It effectively shrinks inflamed tissue, the underlying cause of pain, by improving the blood supply to the area affected. This gummy extract from the Boswella tree is being used on horses and dogs with great success. It acts by mechanism similar to non-steroidal groups of anti-arthritic drugs, with a plus being very few side effects. Dogs with spinal arthritis and hip dysplasia respond favorably when maintenance dosages are given.

•**Bovine cartilage** has become one of the few substances known to man to have healing properties to accelerate clinical cell- growth for skin wounds, torn ligaments, muscle repair, joint deformity and bone degeneration. More concentrated than regular bovine cartilage (ground cartilage), Proteoglycans (bovine cartilage proteins) are effective at treating cancers, arthritis, rheumatism because of its anti-inflammatory properties. The best proteoglycans are found in cows raised organically. After twenty-five years of testing, no side-effects have been recorded.

•**Cat's Claw** (Una de Gato), a rainforest herb that produces oxindole alkaloids proven to enhance phagocytosis (ability of white blood cells and macrophages to attack toxins). An antioxidant, it works to relieve tumors, arthritis, diabetes, allergies, respiratory and circulatory problems, and as an immune booster.

•**Cereal Grass.** Wheat and barley grasses contain all twenty amino-acids, and therefore are a bioavailable source of protein. Dehydrated cereal grasses contain 25% protein, whereas (for an equivalent weight), milk contains 3%, eggs 12% and steak 16%. Vegetable proteins have been considered incomplete (not containing all twenty amino acids). Cereal grass is different according to Pines, manufacturers of wheat and barley grass supplements, claiming they contain all the essential amino acids in amounts which make its protein usable to the body. It also contains high amounts of iron, vitamin C and bioflavonoids.

•**Coenzyme Q10** is found in every food source, including plants, animals and microbes. However, the form of coenzyme Q that is needed for animals comes only from vertebrate sources (Q10) such as mackerel, salmon and sardines. Animals can make their own Q10 from vegetables that contain coenzyme Q9, yeast's Q6, and fungi Q7. Long-term storage of foods can break down these Q enzymes and make them unavailable to the body; therefore, supplementation may be necessary. Coenzyme Q is required for energy production by cells, and is an important antioxidant. It is helpful for heart disease, allergies, periodontal disease, cancer, and to bolster the immune system. Veterinarians use this nutrient to treat chronic skin diseases.

•**Flax** is a superb source of Omega 3 essential fatty acids. These essential fatty acids contribute to a lustrous coat, eliminate hot spots, bald spots, help prevent dry skin, and heal red and raw areas. Flax oil or flax meal are excellent sources of these life-enhancing nutrients.

•**Glucosamine,** is a basal membrane builder known to be an effective treatment for many tissue disorders. It helps restore the thick, gelatinous nature of the fluids and tissues in and around the joints, and is used as treatment for damaged and inflamed muscles, slipped disc, osteoarthritis, and intestinal wall irritations.

•**Hops** are taken from a plant that winds itself around willow and other trees. Hops are known for their antiseptic properties, helping all digestive ailments, general debility and skin eczema. They are also used as natural worming agents, sedatives, appetite stimulants and use of hops may have a definite effect on smooth muscles, particularly that of the digestive tract, being good for chronic bowel disorders.

•**Iodine,** found in sea vegetables, aids digestion and increases assimilation of fatty elements in food. It is know to assist in calcium and phosphorus retention, promoting a better skin and coat condition.

•**Kelp** is a great source of vitamins, iodine, minerals and trace elements, which act as catalysts to aid vital enzyme reactions. It is good for bones, teeth and muscle, brings out the highlights of coat color in older pets, helps arthritic conditions. It is particularly rich in iodine, as well as other essential minerals. It influences the blood, raising the red blood count, and has treated thyroid problems.

•**Lecithin** is a fat burner and promotes alertness, as well as steadying the nerves.

•**Natural-care products.** In addition to feeding your pet healthy food, you should be aware of applications of chemical products that are used to repel fleas, and for grooming. Not all shampoos are good for animals, especially cats, who will lick their fur and ingest the shampoo ingredients. Avoid all shampoos with chemicals in them, and seek out those having nutritional ingredients such as aloe, jojoba oil or herbs. Make sure your flea collar is an herbal type (not chemically based), and never use chemical flea sprays on your pet. To repel fleas, try giving your pets Aged Garlic Extract in their food along with nutritional yeast. This treatment makes their skin emit an odor that is unappealing to fleas. You can also rub the liquid garlic on their skin as a repellent.

•**Nutritional (Bakers') yeast.** Primary (not Brewer's) yeast is a high source of B-vitamins (thiamin, riboflavin, niacin, pyridoxine, Pantothenic acid, biotin and folic acid), amino acids (lysine and tryptophan, which are deficient in grains), and minerals (including molybdenum, chromium and selenium, which are deficient in most diets). Nutritional yeast promotes hair growth, helps in repelling fleas, supports the immune system, and can prevent your dog from blowing coat, even in the summer. Baker's yeast is preferred over Brewer's yeast, because it is grown under carefully controlled conditions on purified mixtures of cane and beet molasses. This allows nutritional uniformity, and produces higher levels of B-vitamins. Brewer's yeast is a by-product of the brewing industry, obtained from sediment left over after fermentation. It is harvested after fermenting as many as ten or eleven batches of beer, and may contain a number of unknown yeast types, some not so healthy.

•**Probiotics** such as Lactobicillus acidophilus, and other probiotics are found naturally in the gastrointestinal tract of healthy animals. These microorganisms provide "friendly" bacteria in the colon to assist with digestion, elimination and restoration of proper flora balance after upset or illness. They also produce lactic acid, and keep the colon environment slightly acid, to prevent the growth of harmful organisms. Environmental, nutritional or situational changes can disrupt and decrease these beneficial micro-organisms in the digestive tract. Without the good bacteria, harmful strains can take over causing intestinal problems. Supplementation may be necessary, especially after usage of drugs, such as beneficial-flora killing antibiotics.

•**Royal Jelly** is the white milky substance produced by worker bees that feed the queen and increase her size sixty percent. Royal jelly contains taurine, an essential nutrient for cats. The effects of royal jelly on animals have included dramatic improvements in arthritic conditions, better coats, relief from insomnia, increased energy and a speedy recovery after surgery. It also contains 10-hydroxy-2-decenoic acid, which has been shown to have powerful antimicrobial characteristics that may enhance the anti-inflammatory effect of royal jelly against arthritis.

•**Seaweeds.** Because foods are becoming nutrient deficient due to ingredient-processing and modern farming practices, seaweeds can provide nutritional tools to help overcome dietary deficiencies. They also provide natural bio-active compounds, with therapeutic health benefits. There are 164 different botanical families of seaweeds, with only 4 of those being kelp. Seaweeds are harvested from the water, dried and then ground into meal. The nutritional quality is affected by the selection of species, as well as the harvesting and drying methods and timing. Since not all seaweed products are the same, request information from the manufacturer as to purity and content. Natural compounds in the seaweeds are undergoing keen scientific investigation for their antiviral, antitumor and immune-potential properties. Seaweeds also contain compounds which enable the body to bind and harmlessly excrete certain toxic heavy metals.

•**Sprirulina.** This planktonic blue-green algae has a sixty-two percent animo acid content, is the world's richest natural source of vitamin B-12, and is different from most algae in that it is easily digested. Scientific studies show that spirulina strengthens the immune system, and causes regression and inhibition of cancers, as well as inhibiting viral replication,. When the cell membrane is attacked by a virus, it normally penetrates it, causing illness. Spirulina prevents this penetration, thereby making the virus unable to reproduce. It is then rendered harmless by the body's defense system. It is also high in GLA essential fatty acid, stimulating growth in animals and making skin and coat shiny and soft. It feeds the beneficial intestinal flora, and is excellent in alleviating symptoms of arthritis. Spirulina is also good at treating parasitic or bacterial infections.

•**Supplements for Hip and Joint problems** have been tested, and results indicate that shark cartilage, calf bone meal, bioflavonoids, rutin, collagen concentrates, antioxidants and minerals are an effective treatment in many degenerative and inflammatory conditions. They provide the building blocks required by the body to repair its own articular cartilage, and reverse the deterioration of connective tissue. It is also thought that combinations of these nutrients can strengthen ligaments, and keep calcium in elemental form so that bone spurs don't occur as hard deposits in the joint.

•**Tea Tree Oil** comes from many sources of trees. The most potent is extracted by steam-distilling from the foliage of the melaleuca alternifolia from New South Wales. Some varieties are labeled organic, some are not. Tea Tree Oil has a high-penetrating ability of skin and mucous membranes, with a low incidence of skin sensitivity. It is antiseptic, antifungal, non-staining, and can also serve as a mild local anesthetic. By stimulating blood flow, it can promote tissue and cell growth, healing a wound. It is useful on skin disorders, including ring worm, helps heal cuts, fungus, repels fleas, and can be used to treat ear infections such as ear mites. Its strong smell disturbs some animals, such as cats, and should not be used where they could lick it off.

•**Velvet Antler.** Humanely harvested from deer and elk, antler velvet has been used for centuries as an aphrodisiac. Most recently, its healing properties have been discovered. Most notable for pets are its anti-inflammatory properties, which facilitate rapid tissue repair after injury. Containing glucosamine and chondroitin sulfate, it helps rebuild cartilage, and improves joint mobility in pets suffering from arthritis. It is useful in cases of anemia, and helps stimulate the formation of red blood cells. Antler velvet improves liver function, and strengthens the immune system.

•**Vitamin C.** Although dogs and cats can manufacture ascorbic acid, the amount produced may not be sufficient to prevent or counteract stresses associated with injury, aging or joint malpositioning. Many animals cannot tolerate high levels of ordinary vitamin C, which can cause gastrointestinal distress. Ester-C contains calcium ascorbate, which permits rapid absorption from the gastrointestinal tract. By reaching higher cellular levels it is excreted more slowly than ordinary vitamin C, and is well tolerated by cats, dogs and horses. A clinical study at Best Friends Animal Sanctuary was performed on dogs given this form of vitamin C. Animals on the Ester-C show marked improvement in mobility in musculoskeletal dysfunction. This additional form of vitamin C is being used to treat animals with arthritis and mobility conditions.

There are stories galore about miracle cures that came from our garden or our pantry (folk remedies). These natural remedies have been used for years on people, and most are equally effective for pets. We have listed our favorites here:

Skin and coat problems:

→ *"I became the adopter of a three-year-old Flat-Coated Retriever bitch on July 24, 1995. When she came to me, she had no hair at all on the back of her legs and her hind-quarters. Her back was red and raw with scabs. She also had a few totally bald patches from scratching, something she did almost incessantly. As you can see from the 'after' photo, in just eight weeks her coat has improved tremendously. The backs of her legs are now feathered, and the redness and scabs have disappeared. I saw improvement almost immediately after beginning feeding her a premium dog food, and adding one and one half scoops of a multi-vitamin, essential fatty acid supplement[29] to her diet. In September 1996, she won an AKC Championship!*

I also use an electrolyte product[30] before shows and during hot weather. It is amazing how "up" the dog stays. I would recommend it highly for anyone who shows their dogs, especially for traveling. It helps to keep the dog from dehydrating, and improves energy as well.
-Terry Ann Fowler, Michigan

Hotspots:
→ *"We have a large colony of rescued greyhounds that serve as blood donors in our not-for-profit blood bank, and then are adopted to pet homes. Some of these greyhounds have low-grade chronic problems with their skin and haircoat (patchy alopecia, thin or brittle hair). For animals showing particular problems, we have been adding a multi-vitamin supplement[31] to their twice-daily feeding, and have seen a significant*

---

[29] NUPRO by Nutri-Pet Research
[30] Custom Electrolyte Formula by Nutri-Pet Research.
[31] Missing Link by Designing Health, Inc.

improvement. Focal areas of hyperemia on the skin have faded, and any irritated 'hotspots' have dried up rapidly. We have also noted improved quality, shine and texture to the coat, and that areas of alopecia have started to grow hair again. Because greyhounds have relatively thin skin that is easily torn, it is important to have their skin in optimum condition to reduce any tendency for scratching, and to promote hair growth."
-W. Jean Dodds, D.V.M., California

Dandruff:

→ *"I have a four and one-half year old English Springer Spaniel named Harry. With proper care, Springers are known to have beautiful soft coats. Unfortunately, they are also prone to dry skin and skin allergies. Harry is no exception. I have tried bathing him with oatmeal baths, tea tree oil, and medicated shampoos. I have tried sprays and lotion, and I brush him daily. This year, his dry skin developed dandruff and a dull, rough coat. The skin on his stomach was bright pink and full of tiny scabs where he'd been scratching and biting.*

On the Internet, I discovered information on a product that contained barley-grass juice powder,[32] and ordered it. Within a few days of giving Harry this powder, his coat was soft and shiny without a speck of dandruff, no more pink stomach or tiny scabs. When I walk him, people actually stop and comment on his beautiful coat. I'm sure the ingredients in the supplement are the reason."
-Elizabeth Narmore, California

Behavioral problems:

→ *"I am a canine behavior specialist, and director of field operations at a local Humane Society. I am always on the lookout for ways to break unwanted behavior in our pets. About a year ago, I started using a herbal calming product[33] that contained valerian, german chamomile, kava kava, St. John's wort and melatonin. This product has turned out to be an excellent addition to my behavior modification tools.*

When people come home and find their house or yard torn up by their dog, they automatically assume the dog is teething or rebelling against them. Many times this has more to do with anxiety attacks. The product reduces anxiety and can help to stop unwanted destructive behavior. I have used this product in conjunction with many training

---

[32] Barley Dog™ by Green Foods Corp.
[33] Happy Traveler™ by Ark Naturals

programs. It works very well with aggression. A lady adopted a Chow from our shelter. She took the dog home and realized the dog wanted to attack her cats. After giving her the supplement, the dog stopped this bad behavior almost immediately. Another client's Siamese cat meowed constantly keeping her up at night. A short dose of the supplement stopped this behavior. I have found it is also useful for pets who are afraid of fireworks and other loud noises."
-Jeff Hoffman, California (www.doggonesmart.com)

Hairballs:
→ *"Both my cats were having a problem with shedding and coughing up frequent hairballs. A friend told me to give them barley grass juice powder.[34] With the first week of daily use of the powder, the results were impressive. Both Rascal and Bandit were much more playful, and their skin and coat looked great, with no 'kitty dandruff'. The shedding and hairballs have become much less frequent. Since the cats are fussy eaters, I wondered if I could get them to eat the powder. So far they like the flavor, and giving them their dosage each morning is no problem."*
-D. Belden, Missouri

Fungus:
→ *"One day a few months ago, I noticed my dog, Nikki, beginning to limp. Upon examining the paw, I found one toe red and swollen, but nothing to indicate what the problem was. I continued to watch her for another few days, as her activity level decreased due to the pain and increased swelling in her toe. We take Nikki to a very progressive and good vet clinic, and they have helped her a lot, but on this visit, the results proved inconclusive. Two days later, she could not even walk on the foot, and refused to move, except when absolutely necessary. The toe had swollen to about the size of her entire foot.*

Upon returning to the vet clinic, they proceeded to cut open the toe for further examination. A small, seed-size lump was found, but I was informed that this was not the cause of the pain and swelling. No real cause for the problem was found. They heavily medicated the paw and wrapped it up. We were given medication and asked to return in two days. She continued to move only as necessary. We returned to the vet clinic in two days, and the bandage was removed. The incision was open wide,

---

[34] Barley Cat™ by Green Foods Corp.

exposing infected tissue and the swelling had not decreased at all. They were baffled!

As a last resort, they would consider removing the toe completely, which is not an uncommon practice in dogs. Our instructions were to put a sock over it to prevent her from licking the incision, continue with antibiotics and keep them informed. We all had been taking aged-garlic extract capsules, but I had heard of amazing healing powers of aged-garlic extract liquid[35]. I decided to try it on Nikki's toe. No one was going to take my dog's toe without a fight.

I soaked a cotton ball with the plain liquid garlic, and held it on the incision for a minute. I also dribbled some in the wound. Then I placed the sock over her foot. I also gave her some garlic extract in a dish to lap up, and I also gave her 6 capsules a day. By the end of the second day, the swelling was going down, and the incision was closing up. By the end of the third day, the incision was completely closed, and the toe was almost its normal size. We returned to the vet clinic five days later, and they were absolutely amazed at the condition of the toe. They had been at a loss for helping Nikki, and were only too pleased that the liquid garlic extract had worked."

Dawn Hoffman, Ohio

Separation anxiety:

→ *"My adopted and presumably abused Lab-Chow mix had problems when people weren't home. We live in a 100 year-old house with beautiful woodworking. Indy would have an anxiety attack when we weren't home, and would chew and claw the woodwork. He ate his way through a three-inch wood front door. I took him to training, locked him in a safe room, fed him just before leaving, and walked him, but nothing worked. There would be damage to the house every time I returned home.*

I then found an herbal, calming supplement[36] used for behavior problems. I first gave it to him in December with good results. I took him off it in January and sure enough, he attacked another door. So, I put him back on it, and he has not destroyed anything in over a month!! The dog balked at first, so we rolled it in balls of bread. He gleefully eats the bread and doesn't notice the supplement."

-Marc Roland

---

[35] Kyolic® Aged Garlic Extract™ by Wakunaga of America, Co., Ltd.
[36] Happy Traveler™ by Ark Naturals

A report from the Aequus Veterinary Service reported the following success with antioxidants and vitamins:

→ *CASE 1: 16 yr. old Persian-mix cat.*

Complaint: Difficulty walking, anorexia, weight loss, irritable personality

Exam: Marked loss of range of motion in both coxofemoral joints, decreased lateral motion of most lumbar vertebrae, poor, dry hair coat, 20% below ideal weight; abdominal palpation revealed kidneys slightly small and firm.

Treatment: Cat was adjusted in lumbosacral area, all lumbars and lower cervicals. Owner was recommended to put cat on raw-meat diets with vegetables and grains. The only supplement cat was placed on was Vetri-Science Nu-Cat feline vitamins with additional supplementation with 400 IU Vitamin E.

Response: Owner reported that cat was markedly better within a week in both its activity level and appetite. At 3 months, an exam reported the cat continues to progress well. Hair coat has improved dramatically, and cat's attitude is much improved. She wants to be part of the family again. Acupuncture has been added to the treatment regimen.

→ *CASE 4: 13 yr. old domestic short hair cat*

Complaint: Kidney failure, anorexia, emaciation, stiffness

Exam: Cat showed 15-20% loss of ideal body weight. Skin is dry and dull with dander flakes. Approximately 8% dehydration was estimated. During crisis last summer, veterinarian recommended euthanasia. Cat was eating only tuna at time of exam.

Treatment: Owner was taught how to administer subcutaneous saline fluids to maintain hydration. Cat was acupunctured every other day for two weeks for renal failure. Severe nutritional compromise was also diagnosed due to diet. Cat was found to eat vegetable/meat baby foods (organic origin) and was put on them. Added to the diet were blue-green algae, Vetri-Science LinoPrim (essential fatty acid Evening Primrose Oil) and Vetri-Science Cell Advance 440.

Response: Cat has improved considerably, considering the severe degenerative state that the cat is in. He now talks to the owners, comes to meals with other cats and is more willing to interact. The cat's coat color has deepened, and dander is resolving. Owners are reasonable about expectations and are not trying for a cure, but improvement in this cat shows importance of maintaining proper nutrition. Cat is slowly putting on weight.

Regarding bee pollen:

→ *DeeDee Jonrowe, a top racer in the Iditarod and Alpirod races for sled dogs, feeds bee pollen to her champion team.*

Success with garlic and wheat grass supplements:

→ *"My eight-month old puppy had an extremely severe skin condition. He had sores all over his body and hardly any hair, and he was so sore he did not want to even move. He had even given up scratching, as it was too uncomfortable. He was so sick that we did not think he would make it through the night. A friend advised us to give him some wheat grass powder[37]. We also added enzymes and minerals to his regime. I mixed the contents with water and syringed the concoction into the pup's mouth several times throughout the day. I also had made up a solution of the minerals and enzymes, along with some aged garlic extract,[38] and sponged that over all the sores and pustules. He made it through the night, and the next day he had only a mild fever. Within several days, he was up and dashing about. A week later, his skin is healing beautifully and his appetite is back."*
-Jeanne Vuyosevich, Farmingdale,N.J.

A three-pound Pom's life saved by acidophilus:

→ *" I have recently had a three pound Pom pick up a virus and I couldn't control the diarrhea until I managed to get down two capsules of a probiotic supplement[39] on a bit of baby food. I had to nurse her round the clock to be sure she took fluids (by eyedropper), and sneak in a little bit of the baby food. I had nursed her for forty-eight hours without success in stabilizing the bowel and stomach. After giving her the probiotics, she settled down for a good four hours before a normal bowel movement. I continued its usage for a week, and each day she continued to improve. I believe it helped to save my 'Schweet's' life. A three-pound Pom doesn't have much luck surviving after two or three days of dehydration and diarrhea. She's fat and happy again, and trying to rule the roost."*
-Toni Dickerson, Maryland

---

[37] Pines Wheat Grass, Pines International
[38] Kyolic® Liquid Aged Garlic Extract™ by Wakunaga of America Co., Ltd.
[39] Kyo-dophilus™, by Wakunaga of America Co., Ltd.

A testimonial to essential fatty acid supplements:

→*"One of our customers had such great results using flaxseed[40] for her arthritis, that she gave it to her dog who had a terrible fungus. She found it worked so well that his hair stopped falling out in clumps, and the fungus disappeared. A plus was that his coat became more shiny and beautiful than before. Our dog, Tasha, was troubled with severe diarrhea, so I tried the flax, and by the next morning, the problem was gone. Some letters we have received from users who have given it to their pets, said they become more energetic with the flaxseed."*

-Milly Nelson, Wisconsin

Usage of various substances comes from the Anne Arundel Veterinary Hospital in Maryland:

→ *A three-year-old male yellow Labrador was seen in May of 1993 for diarrhea. The dog proved negative for hook worms, but ulcerative colitis was suspected. The dog was treated, unsuccessfully, with a sulfonamide drug Flagyl® Lomotil® and a diet of Hills Prescription Diet® Canine W/D®. In August of 1995, the dog was started on a supplement containing N-Acetyl Glucosamine.[41] Six months have passed and the dog has only had one episode of diarrhea.*

Common hip dysplasia:

→*"Winston is a twelve year old Springer Spaniel, who had lost a lot of his "spring". Four years ago, he was operated on for OCD bone chips in his elbow. Then three years ago, his X-rays showed moderate hip dysplasia. By then, his suffering had increased so intensely that there were periods when he cried every morning when he tried to get up out of bed. Once or twice a week, he would refuse to get up at all.*

The vets I contacted gave little hope. They said my options were shots of pain-killing steroids, or hip replacement surgery. I wasn't willing to believe that nothing else could be done, so I started working with naturopathic health-care professionals. We settled on a combination of imported New Zealand Shark tissue concentrates, Vitamin C, Pantothenic acid, and bromelaine, along with vitamin A, E, minerals, collagen concentrate, calf bone meal, lemon bioflavonoids, rutin, helperidan and herbs. After the first month of treatment, Winston complained about

---

[40] Fortified Flax, Omega Life, Inc.

[41] Vetri-Science Multi-Source Glucosamine®, Vetri-Science Laboratories.

getting up only once. He now has a whole new gait. The "spring" is back in his step. The results were so immediate, the relief so obvious, that we started giving 'Winston's Formula[42]' to other dog owners, with equally as dramatic results.

Winston had been on a one-a-day treatment for three months. Now, we have cut back to a maintenance level of every other day or every third day. We will keep this up for the rest of his life. He will never by 'cured', but from the look on his face, he certainly has 'healed'.
-Mark Sherman, California

•NON-TRADITIONAL APPROACHES TO HEALING

Tachyonized energy

Tachyon energy, otherwise known as life-force energy, is not a specific nutrient, yet it has been proven to have an integral part in the healing realm. When it is blocked, our electrical system can short-circuit, and prevent healing. From experience, we know that we can clear such blocks by using high quality organic foods, natural supplements, essences, and now with the newly developed life-force energy antennae.

Photo by Star Dewar

For the first time in history, we have scientific methods of restructuring certain materials at the sub-molecular level that then become antennae that attract and focus usable biological energy—Tachyon energy. These tools provide the energy needed to begin the balancing process from the inside out. This is not a fanciful theory, but rather a conceptual revelation, taking root worldwide, as the rejuvenating benefits of Tachyon energy are demonstrated on a global scale.

→ *"Paulette, a friend of mine's thirteen-year-old Golden Lab, was diagnosed with pancreatic failure, and given only one week to live. My heart was open as I held my friend in my arms, and we both cried. I didn't see Paulette for almost two months, and when I did, I couldn't believe my eyes! The dog was perfectly healthy. My friend told me that she had used Tachyon water drops in Paulette's mouth and put large Tachyon cells in*

---
[42] Winston's Joint Formula, The Pet Project

her bed as well as a cell taped onto her collar, and her dog recovered. I have tried this technique on other animals since then, with great success."
-Shari Lynn, California

→ *"They call me Mr. Sat, and I am a handsome nineteen-year-old terra-cotta Tabby cat. I admit that I owe my excellent health and good looks to something my mom started experimenting with three years ago, Tachyon Energy. First our water was energized, then we got a Tachyonized Life Pad to sleep on, and Tachyon pendants on our collars. It seemed to be working, but the proof came when mom brought home a very skinny stray cat. She had a raggedy coat and runny eyes. I thought to myself, 'good grief, could that grundgy look be contagious?' Next thing I knew, mom put Tachyonized Water right into her mouth. After only two weeks, the little orphaned Annie's fur started to shine like the rest of us. The bald spots filled in with downy fur. Her leaky eyes cleared up, and she was no longer an embarrassment. It was that simple; just a few drops on top of her food morning and night.*

In the fall, we all rejoiced, because not one of us, including the dogs, suffered one bit from the usual dry, itching, hot spots that had plagued us for years at the end of summer. The only thing different in our diets was the Tachyonized Water! It was about that time that our neighbor's cat Moe, got the Tachyon treatment. One night he was sprayed in the face by an offended skunk, and could hardly breathe. His owner thought of taking him to the clinic, but decided to call our house, wanting to try the Tachyon Water drops first. His nose, throat and lung inflammation cooled quickly.

Photo Star Dewar

The Tachyonized Life Capsule that she hung from his collar accel-erated his complete recovery, and he still wears it every day. Even my sweetheart, Essence of Pearl, was helped. She was tired and thin, and had begun experiencing seizures. We were told that she had almost no red blood cells, and the vet thought the end was near. She was given Tachyonized Silica Gel daily, and after a few days showed her same old interest in food. Within four weeks, she was taken back to the vet's office and shocked them all—her blood was back to normal! The miracle of Tachyon has certainly enhanced the quality of life around here."
-Star Dewar, for Mr. Sat of California

Magnets

Magnets have been used for centuries to heal all sorts of ailments. The earth and all bodily cells have magnetic fields that function within a normal range. Various conditions can upset the magnet balance in our bodies. Using magnet therapy may restore this balance. They seem to heal the body by removing inflammation and restoring circulation. By increasing blood flow to a damaged area, needed nutrients are delivered to that site for healing. They also have the ability to reverse toxic acids, helping to restore the body to a normal alkaline state.

When you apply magnets, they are specific to the area that needs the increased blood flow and oxygen delivery. Pet pads (for sleeping) magnets penetrate 4 ½" into the animal's body. Magnet collars work on the theory of surrounding an area to affect the body's entire circulatory system. When you create a circle (as in a collar), the magnetic field that forms inside that circle dilates the blood vessels, thus increasing the blood cells' capacity to carry oxygen. Because eventually all blood cells pass through the area within the collar, the entire body receives the positive effects without having a magnet directly applied to problem areas.

Magnets appear to have no negative side effects, although warnings insist that they not be used on pregnant animals. Manufacturers are constantly receiving letters of thanks whereby magnets were used in treating arthritis, pain, post-surgery recovery and lethargy. A few of them are listed here:

→ *"I recently purchased magnet pet collars for our nine-year old poodles, both suffering from osteoarthritis. Our veterinarian had tried the shots on both dogs for three months in a row. They both had bad reactions to the medication, and it had to be stopped. Within two days of putting the magnet collars[43] on, they both were running around like they were five years younger. The results are great, and this is very exciting for us, and for Muffy and Pooh."*
-David Pratt, North Carolina

---

[43] Magnetic Therapy Pet Collar by The Gem Stem, Inc.

It is necessary to understand that indoor pets have a list of health hazards that may not be recognized. Have you ever bought a new carpet in the winter? Did you install it and then go off and lock your pets in the house? New carpets contain 2000 chemicals, many of them carcinogenic. Your pets will try to avoid these chemical fumes and jump on the furniture. They are trying to tell you something! Chemical fumes from furnishings, carpets and drapery settle within two feet of the floor. Since this is where your pets spend most of their time, it is extremely important to change your idea about decorating materials.

There are numerous books on the subject of indoor air and non-toxic furnishings. We suggest that you educate yourself to protect the health of your pet. We have listed some specific hazards here and will attempt to give you safe alternatives.

•HEALTHY DRINKING WATER.

You may wonder why we discuss water as an essential element that is in short supply in the body. Pets, especially indoor pets, depend on their owners to provide them with enough water for optimum health. This sounds simple, but how often do our hectic lives get in the way of remembering to fill their water dish, or at least checking it several times a day to see if it's empty. Animals being fed dry food may suffer from dehydration, as dry food contains only 12% moisture, as opposed to about an 80% moisture content that would be found in the wild or in canned food.

Not only should pet owners be conscious of providing ample water for their pet, but they should determine if the water is pure. Acid rain, pesticides, agricultural runoff, and industrial pollution tend to change the constitution of our water sources, not only making it hazardous to drink, but mixing many bad minerals (lead, mercury, cadmium) with the good. Too bad for the wild animals, but you give your pet tap water which has to be better—right?

Wrong! Tap water has been chlorinated, fluoridated, and treated, which removes many minerals. Those that remain may not be bioavailable (able to be absorbed by the body), therefore it is necessary to add back electrolyte trace minerals in the form of a supplement. Unfiltered tap water can also pick up bacteria on its way to your sink, and may not be healthy to drink. Well water is probably better, but then again, environmental pollution or agricultural runoff could be sending hazardous water to your well. Your solution may include drinking bottled water or filtered water, but do you give it to your pets, or are they still relegated to tap water?

Several methods of home water treatment are available. Whole-house filters can be installed, or you can use counter-top or under the sink point-of-use filters on your faucet. Carbon, KDF and other types of filters are available to remove many contaminants, although Reverse Osmosis units will take out 98% of the dissolved solids, and Distillation will remove 100%. Whichever method you decide upon, please make sure your pet receives the same pure water as you drink. Since reverse osmosis or distillation removes many of the minerals, it is important to add a liquid mineral supplement with electrolytes, to your water, or face many of the diseases caused by deficiencies. The two most important health devices you should invest in are a water-filtration system, and an air-purification device.

•CLEAN AIR

Indoor pets have a distinctive disadvantage over outdoor animals. They depend on humans to provide them with fresh air to breathe. That could be a big mistake, as most pet owners are not even aware of the need for clean air in their homes. Many people, and pets too, suffer from allergies. Many of these come from airborne pathogens, mold, dust and out-gassing chemical fumes from carpets, cleaners, stain-resistant fabrics and other decorating materials which you may not have know are even hazardous. In some cases, our homes become toxic gas chambers for the animals we love. Outdoor pets may be at risk if you live in an area of high air pollution, but statistics show that indoor air, potentially can be dirtier than outside city air.

The problem is creating a healthy indoor air environment for you and your pets. The solution is simple. Install one of the many types of air cleaners or air purifiers being sold today. Ozone-generating machines are effective against dust, mold, bacteria, airborne pathogens and chemicals. If these units contain an ionizer, they create an atmosphere similar to the calming effect noticed after a thundershower passes. This negative ionization of the air tends to calm pets. The ozone also tends to kill certain bacteria that may cause skin reactions, and make animals scratch or birds peck their feathers. Electronic air-filters are effective against dust and also animal dander, mold fragments and odors. High efficiency particulate arrestor (HEPA) filters and carbon filters have been combined in many units and are also extremely effective at keeping the air indoors fresh and clean. Whichever type of unit you decide is best, for your pet's sake, make this purchase a priority.

Air exchange is also important. Heat recovery ventilators and air exchangers are offered in homes under construction, but if you have a well-insulated home with no mechanical means of getting the air in, then open a window from time to time. The fresh air is definitely worth the price you pay for a little heat loss.

→ *"A friend of mine had a dog boarding kennel which had good ventilation in the summer, but when winter came she had to close the windows. She noticed the animals who were residents of longer than a week exhibited signs of depression, or became irritable. She also had a high rate of watery eyes and sniffles, even though she kept the place immaculate. She thought the problem might stem from the stuffy air, and started investigating air-purification systems. She decided upon a unit that uses ozone to clean the air.[44] This seemed to stop the drippy eyes and sniffles, and she also noticed her animals calmed down and seemed happier.*

The manufacturer's representative told her it was probably due to the ion generator that was part of the unit. It seems that in the winter static electricity builds up inside buildings, creating positive ions. These have a negative effect on emotions. Once the air purifier started delivering both positive and negative ions, a balance was created and the static electricity diminished, along with the depression and anxiety. It also helped her business, because the pets went home without the kennel cough or nervous behavior normally associated with a stay in a boarding facility."
B.R., Massachusetts

•LIGHT

Outdoor animals don't have the problem of the SAD syndrome (seasonal affective disorder), but indoor pets do. Just like people, light plays an important part in the mood of an animal. Being deprived of natural sunlight, such as we find in many homes and apartments, can affect the health of your dog and cat. And we wonder why they are restless and mope so much! Lack of sunlight can cause functional disorders of the nervous

---

[44] Alpine Air Purifer

system, a vitamin D deficiency, a weakening of the body's defenses and an aggravation of chronic diseases.

Light is a nutrient, similar to all the other nutrients we take in through food, and we need the full range of natural daylight. This is a fact, long since proven by science. If you have enough sunny windows, dogs and cats will find their way to the "light". If your apartment or house primarily faces east or north, sunlight may not enter the living space in enough quantities to provide proper amounts of Vitamin D. If this is the case, you should supplement your indoor environment with full-spectrum light bulbs, which mimic sunlight. Available for many years as 'grow' lights for plants, these bulbs come in a variety of shapes and sizes to fit your lighting fixture.

Photo by Neil Shively

•UNSUSPECTING HAZARDS

<u>Cat Litter</u>. Although this is not a nutrient, we include it because using the wrong litter can definitely cause illness in your cat or ferret. Seventy-one percent of cat owners keep a litter box in their house. A majority of this is clay litter, which is not biodegradable, and may cause sneezing and/or allergies in animals due to the dust created when they use it. Most of these litters do not cause anything more than an inconvenience, as the animal tracks them around the house, but some can cause illness, and even death. The biggest hazard to pet health from litter is from the clumping varieties. Although convenient for disposal purposes, most clumping litter contains forty to one hundred percent of Sodium Bentonite as an agent, which swells to fifteen times its original size after absorbing moisture.

When cats ingest or inhale this substance, this litter expands inside their body, forming a mass and coating its interior, causing dehydration and preventing the absorption of nutrients or fluids. When it coats the digestive tract, it attracts the collection of old fecal matter, increasing toxicity, bacterial growth and prohibiting proper absorption of digested food. This can lead to stress on the immune system and promote illness, including viral, bacterial, parasitic and yeast infections, which may result in death. This agent acts as an expandable cement, and therefore it should never be flushed down plumbing. -Tiger Tribe, Nov. 1994 and Holistic Animal Care, 1994

Taking this statement one step further, it has been found that in cats using this type of clumping litter, their digestive tracts became plugged (just like plumbing), and they die because of blockage. There is an alternative type of clumping litter on the market that uses Guar as the clumping agent. It swells a minimal amount when it absorbs moisture, and then begins to dissolve. Therefore, it is able to pass through the digestive tract (and plumbing). One manufacturer only uses two percent of Guar in their litter, therefore it is considered safe. Please, for the life of your litter-bound pet, read labels carefully and do not use Sodium Bentonite-based clumping litter.

New to the market are silica litters. These have high absorption and reduce odors. Some veterinarians advise using this type of litter, while others warn about silica absorption causing health hazards. More research is being done on the safety of these litters. The biggest problem with many of them is that they are shaped like little balls, and roll all over your floor when the cat tracks them out of the litter box. We have used these litters, and find them uncanny in their ability to roll away and avoid getting swept up in the dust pan. Alternatives are cedar, recycled newspaper, corn, pelleted grasses, particulate wheat, plant fiber or wood fiber. Most of these, especially corn and wheat, easily biodegrade back into the soil and pose no health hazard to your cat.

→ *"I have had cats for 30 years, and have used every kind of litter imaginable. Luckily, I discovered the hazards of clumping litter containing sodium bentonite after I had been using it only a short time and I went back to the clay litter. Unfortunately, we have to dispose of this in a plastic bag that we take to the dump ourselves. This became increasingly inconvenient. A friend of mine introduced us to a corn litter[45] that had the consistency of wheat germ. It was a clumping litter and unless my cats pooped, the litter never smelled. This litter also was biodegradable so I could dump it in the back of my yard and mix it into the soil. I feel so much better that I am using environmentally friendly litter, and that it is not causing any harm to my animals."*
-C.T., Westport, CT.

---

[45] World's Best Cat Litter

Shots. I was advised by a holistic vet not to vaccinate my cat for feline leukemia, because studies have shown that trauma is caused at the site of the injections, many times leading to cancerous growths. He told me to keep her immune system strong with proper diet and nutrient supplements, and most likely I wouldn't have to worry about this dreaded disease. I took his advice. People with pets whose immune systems are compromised, and who aren't on a good nutrition regime, may not have been willing to take this risk.

Veterinarians agree that vaccinations can cause a variety of problems in animals, but they disagree as to the breadth and severity of their reactions. Illnesses that were contracted after shots were given may not necessarily be related to the vaccination. Some breeds react more strongly than others to vaccinations, such as Rottweilers, Harlequin Great Danes, Akitas and Weimaraners. Many animals develop urinary-tract infections after their annual shots, especially when more than one type is given during the procedure. Tumors that develop at the site of the injection is another "side effect". Since vaccinations are supposed to mimic the process of diseases, causing the body to produce antibodies, minuscule amounts of the actual virus must be injected. This is unnatural.

Normally, infectious diseases travel a route through the body, allowing the immune system to kick in at various stages. Injections bypass this normal routing, and short-circuit the very important primary response mechanisms. We have placed the virus directly into the blood, and given it free and immediate access to the major immune organs and tissues, without any obvious way of getting rid of it. Added to the assault are the many carriers added to the vaccine, such as aluminum sulfate, mercuric oxide, formaldehyde, artificial colors, antibiotics, BHA and BHT or other chemicals. In real life, most animals will not experience attacks from multiple diseases at the same time, although we give our pets multi-shot treatments during their annual visit to the vet. Animals with weak immune systems will be at risk for either developing these diseases, or contracting associated illness.

Many skin problems have been shown to develop from vaccinations, as well as arthritic conditions and degenerative spinal diseases. Rabies vaccines are known to cause personality changes, skin changes, damage to the thyroid and endocrine systems, and lowered immunity. The side effects are not worth the risk if there are alternatives. Homeopathic nosodes, inactive virus essences, are now being used instead of vaccinations. They can be an effective alternative, and have few side effects, as they are more synergistic with the body, but if an animal is immune-compromised, they will still be subject to getting the disease, which is true for vaccinations as well. An alternative, as we mentioned before, is to fortify your pet's immune system through proper nutrition. Professional homeopaths also prescribe a single, specific remedy, based upon the totality of the individual symptoms, to assist the defense mechanism in overcoming a developing disease. If given immediately after exposure to a known disease, nosodes can prevent the development of clinical disease, and even the dreaded feline leukemia responds well to this type of treatment.

I personally am using homeopathic nosodes in place of feline leukemia vaccinations, and especially for my kitty who has the HIV virus. If you would like more information on this type of disease prevention, contact Dr. Stephen Tobin, D.M.V. in Meridan, Connecticut. He has been working with homeopathic vaccinations for years, and is a prominent figure with the Holistic Veterinary Medical Association. Dr.Tobin is available for consultations at (203) 238-9863.

Toxic flea treatments: Everyone hates fleas, and will go to great lengths to keep them away. In fact, it is considered a necessary service to keep pets as free of fleas as possible. Unfortunately, as is the case with other pest control methods, many of the substances that are marketed as beneficial to pets actually can bring serious harm to them.

Pyrethrum is a nontoxic insecticide made from chrysanthemum flowers, and used as a flea repellent. It is considered safe in its natural state, and reactions usually are limited to increased salivation because of pyrethrum's bitter taste, although it can be harmful to frogs and reptiles. However, many pyrethrum products contain chemical additives that are dangerous for dogs and cats, causing such symptoms as vomiting, diarrhea, mild tremors, hyperexcitability, severe hypersalivation, depression and seizures. These symptoms usually last for up to three days, unless the animal is re-exposed. Read labels carefully and use only natural pyrethrum powders.

One popular ingredient in insect repellents for humans is diethyl toluamide (DEET). It is estimated that 22% of the general population in the United States is exposed to DEET-based products annually, especially mosquito repellents. This substance can also be found in some flea repellents. Certain symptoms related to nervous disorders can arise with repeated use of DEET on pets. Furthermore, in 1990, the Washington Toxic Coalition (Dorman, District of Columbia) reported that cats have died from repeated flea baths containing DEET. Cats and dogs develop tremors, vomiting, excitation, and seizures. This substance has been proven to penetrate the skin of guinea pigs within six hours, and may cause problems with the central nervous system. Human children can also be affected, exhibiting signs of lethargy, behavioral changes, abnormal movements, seizures and coma, as well as chemical burns to sensitive skin. It is safest to choose a less toxic alternative.

Chemical flea collars pose a threat to small animals. Some contain DDVP that is supposedly non-toxic for dogs, but sensitive animals can suffer excessive salivation, diarrhea and respiratory difficulties due to this substance. The constant inhalation of DDVP fumes can cause permanent damage to internal organs. And remember, as the size of the animal decreases, the risk of toxic-effects increases. Flea collars that include dichlorvos among their ingredients may cause contact dermatitis in some pets. In addition, commercial flea collars use chemicals that claim to kill the pests, but fleas often hop over the collars and inhabit the pet's face. Therefore, you may be exposing your pet to harmful chemicals that don't even serve their purpose! Most chemical flea collars come with warnings about their toxicity. But, the whole story isn't told: "dust from this collar is harmful if swallowed, and may cause eye problems"; "if not removed from pets during baths, make sure shampoo contaminated with collar dust does not get into the eyes"; "follow disposal directions properly."

Foggers or "bombs" are often used to eliminate fleas that have infested the home. Warnings on these products indicate that the fumes are dangerous and that the mist, which settles over the area, is harmful when inhaled or when absorbed through the skin; food and cooking surfaces should be covered; aquariums and plants should be protected prior to use. Instructions state that people and pets should vacate the home during use, but may return after the fumes have dissipated. However, the chemicals used in flea bombs have half-lives of more than fifty years. Therefore, if foggers are employed, you will be living with toxins inside of your home, and so will the next owner of the house. Active ingredients in foggers include DDVP, propoxur, diazinon, and carbaryl, all of which are nerve poisons to both pets and humans. Their residues remain in furnishings, carpets, and drapes. Unfortunately, despite this assault on your house, the fleas don't stay away! Repeated "bombings" are necessary, increasing the chance for sickness each time.

Alternatives are to look for natural flea collars and repellents that use herbs. We recommend preventive measures that include boosting the animal's immune system. Fleas are more attracted to weak animals, and by keeping your pet in top shape, fleas will choose another animal. Nutritional yeast is a superb supplement to give your animal along with garlic (preferably an aged-garlic supplement). The B-vitamins in the nutritional yeast, and the garlic seem to create a certain skin odor which fleas don't like. We have used this method for years, with great success.

Hazardous plants: Animals tend to consume plants as a natural way to improve their health. For example, cats normally eat grass for nutrition, as well as to induce vomiting for the removal of hairballs. There are many cases in which pets accidentally ingest toxins from poisonous plants, result in sickness. Common indoor and outdoor plants can cause illness, and in extreme cases, death. Cats may scratch plants and become infected when grooming their claws. Dogs may randomly chew or eat plants that emit intriguing scents. Therefore, it is important to be familiar with the types of plants in your area, and to keep the toxic ones out of your pets' paths.

Catnip is an example of a relatively harmless plant that simply intoxicates the kitty. But, other common house and yard plants have lethal effects on our animal friends. The best way to prevent plant poisoning is to familiarize yourself with common dangerous plants, and to either remove them from the premises, or carefully monitor you pet's favorite spot.

Irritating plants commonly cause skin rashes—allergic dermatitis—in both pets and humans. If your animal develops a skin condition, trace his or her "haunts" to determine if a toxic plant may be causing the problem. You might not be able to identify harmful plants yourself, but observe the vegetation and report anything that you find suspicious or unfamiliar to the veterinarian. As with all symptomatic conditions, the veterinarian will be able to offer better treatment if he or she knows the entire story.

Symptoms of plant poisoning:

• Breathing difficulties	• Skin rash
• Convulsions	• Stomach upset
• Excessive salivation	• Swallowing with difficulty
• Gastroenteritis	• Vomiting
• Irritation of mouth and lips	• Watery eyes and nose

Indoor plants can be as poisonous as they are pretty. Dieffenbachia inflames the mouth and lips of some dogs and cats. It may also interfere with breathing and swallowing. Philodendron has been known to cause irritation of the mucous membranes and excessive salivation in cats. Daffodils and Indian rubber plants are also toxic. Dried flower arrangements are a beautiful addition to a home's decor, but often contain toxic plants. Hydrangea and bittersweet have been known to provoke gastroenteritis. Furthermore, the ingestion of bittersweet can result in unconsciousness

Plants are a common form of holiday decoration. While you are preparing festive arrangements, know which species are dangerous to your pet. Mistletoe, if eaten, can be lethal to a dog. Poinsettias may cause vomiting, and even death to any household pet. Even Christmas tree needles and the water from the base of the tree can provoke gastrointestinal distress. Easter lilies are poisonous to cats. We have listed many of the common toxic plants in the chart below:

Poisonous Plants (partial list):

Indoor Plants		Outdoor Plants	
Bittersweet		Daphne	
Dieffenbachia		Holly	
Easter lilies		Hyacinth bulbs	
Indian rubber plant		Iris	
Hydrangea		Lantanas	
Mistletoe		Laurel	
Philodendron		Lily of the Valley	
Poinsettias		Rhododendron	
Pine needles		Tiger lilies	
Leaves from:			
Avocado	Rhubarb	Spinach	Tomato
Seeds from:			
Apple	Black Locust	Cherry	Elderberry
Oak	Peach		

Symptoms and Sources of Pet Poisoning: The following table lists a number of symptoms, and identifies toxic sources that may be causing each of them. If your pet is experiencing any of these symptoms, try to eliminate the source of the poison. If the condition is extreme, contact your veterinarian immediately, or the National Animal Poison Control Center listed at the end of this chapter.

Symptoms	Pet	Possible Source
Aimless running	Dogs	lead poisoning
Anorexia	Cats	pesticides, flea repellents, contaminated water
	Dogs	lead, pesticides, flea repellents, contaminated water
Anxiety	Cats/Dogs	building/decorating materials, cleaning products
Asthma	Cats/Dogs	cleaning products
Blindness	Dogs	lead
Breathing Problems	Cats/Dogs	building/decorating materials, carbon monoxide, cleaning products, pesticides, flea repellents, toxic plants
Burns (mouth)	Cats/Dogs	cleaning products
Cardiac arrhythmia	Cats/Dogs	cleaning products
Chomping of jaws	Dogs	lead
Confusion	Cats/Dogs	carbon monoxide
Convulsions	Cats/Dogs	carbon monoxide, lead, pesticides, flea repellents, toxic plants
Cough	Cats/Dogs	building/decorating materials, cleaning products, mold, dust
Depression	Cats/Dogs	building/decoration materials, pesticides, flea repellents, lack of sunlight
Diarrhea	Cats/Dogs	cleaning products, pesticides and flea repellents
Distemper behavior	Dogs	water contamination
Excessive salivation	Cats/Dogs	cleaning products, toxic plants
Foaming at mouth	Cats/Dogs	cleaning products, pesticides and flea repellents
Gastric upset	Cats	lead, contaminated water
	Dogs	contaminated water
Gastroenteritis	Cats/Dogs	pesticides, flea repellents, toxic plants
Hair loss	Cats	cleaning products
Hysteria	Cats	lead
Indiscriminate biting	Dogs	lead
Irritability	Cats/Dogs	building/decoration materials, carbon monoxide, pesticides, flea repellents
Mouth irritation	Cats/Dogs	toxic plants
Nervousness	Cats/Dogs	building/decorating materials, pesticides, flea repellents
Panting	Cats	cleaning products
Restlessness	Cats/Dogs	cleaning products, lead, contaminated water
Seizures	Cats/Dogs	cleaning products, pesticides, flea repellents

Symptoms	Pet	Possible Source
Shortness of breath	Cats/Dogs	carbon monoxide
Skin rash	Cats/Dogs	building/decorating materials, contaminated water
Stiffness	Cats/Dogs	pesticides
Swallowing Difficulty	Cats/Dogs	toxic plants
Vomiting	Cats/Dogs	carbon monoxide, cleaning products, pesticides, flea repellents, toxic plants, contaminated water
Watery eyes & nose	Cats/Dogs	toxic plants
Whining & growling	Dogs	lead

If you are in a panic because you think your pet has been poisoned and you are unable to get to a veterinarian immediately, you can contact the ASPCA's National Animal Poison Control Center. It is the first animal-oriented poison center in the United States. The center's phones are answered by licensed veterinarians and board certified veterinary toxicologists. Do not call your local human poison control center, as they are not well-versed in treatments for pets. The National Animal Poison Control Center has extensive experience with over 250,000 cases involving plants, pesticides, drugs, metals, and other toxic exposures that have harmed pets and food-producing animals. There is a charge for consultation. For emergencies call (900) 680-0000 ($20 for the first 5 minutes + $2.95 ea. additional minute charged to your phone bill). Or you can pay by credit card at $30.00 per case by calling (800) 548-2423 or (888) 4-ANI-HELP.

National Animal Poison Control Center
1717 South Philo Rd.
Urbana IL, 61802
(217) 333-5310

EPILOGUE

We've provided you with a lot of food for thought, and some pretty interesting stories. Hopefully, you will take most of this information to heart. Our kitties and pooches are victims of over-zealous, money-hungry pet-food manufacturers, chemical company opportunists and complacent pet owners. There are good people out there who are trying to give your pets a fighting chance at a long and healthy life. We're cheering for them and so are your animals. Hopefully, much of the information presented in this book has touched your heart enough to spark you to do more research. Appendix A lists companies that produce critter-friendly products. Write to them for more information. The smarter you get about your pet's health, the longer they will remain alive and healthy, as loving members of your family.

INDEX

• BIBLIOGRAPHY

•*Are Your Pets Getting A Well-Balanced Meal?*, Better Nutrition, August. 1995

•Anderson, Nina & Peiper, Howard, *Are You Poisoning Your Pets?*, Safe Goods, 1995

•Balch, James M.D. Balch, Phyllis A. C.N.C. *Prescription for Nutritional Healing*, Avery Pub. Group Inc., 1990.

•Belay, A., Ota Y., Miyakawa K., Shimamatsu H., *Current knowledge on potential health benefits of Spirulina*, Journal of Applied Phycology 5:235-241, 1993

•Brown, L. Phillips, DVM, *Ester-C For Joint Discomfort - A Study*, Natural Pet, Nov.-Dec., 1994

•Burton Goldburg Group, *Alternative Medicine* Puyallup, Washington: Future Medicine Pub.,1993

•Chalem, Jack, *Medical Journal Document Value of Bee Propolis, Honey, and Royal Jelly*, Natural Foods Merchandiser, July 1995

•Cichoke, Dr. A.J., *The Best in Natural Pet Care*, Health Food Business, July 1995

•Dorosz, Edmund, DVM, *Specialty Diets*, Natural Pet, Nov.-Dec. 1995

•Dunn, T.J., Jr., D.V.M., *Food For Thought*, DOG World, April, 1995

•Dworkin, Norine, *Good Eats*, Natural Pet, Dec. 1996

•Erasmus, Udo, *Healing Fats for Animals (and us)*, Natural Pet p.36, Sep/Oct 1995

•Finn, Kathleen *Just Rinse Those Troubles Away.* Delicious Magazine, Mar. 1995, p.15.

•Garland, Anne Witte with Mothers and Others, *The Way We Grow*, Berkley Books, 1993.

•Hanger, Sylla Sheppard, *Vegetal Oils and Additives*, The Aromatherapy Practioner Reference Manual, reprinted Natural Pet, Jan/Feb 1996

•*Healthy Nutrition*, DENES Natural Pet Care Limited Advisory Svc., E Sussex, U.K.

•Holt, James S., *The Organic Foods Production Act* Organic Foods Production Association of North America, The Organic Food Alliance, 1990.

•Jennings, J.B., *Feeding, Digestion and Assimilation in Animals*, MacMillian Press, Ltd., 1972

•Jones, Cris, *Feeding Senior Dogs*, Natural Pet, p. 57, Jan/Feb 1996

•Kirschmann, Gayla J. and Kirschmann, John D., *Nutrition Almanac*, McGraw Hill, 1996.

•Kohnke, John, B.V.Sc., R.D.A., *Feeding And Nutrition, The Making of A Champion*, Birubi Pacific, 1992

•Kostecki, Henry, D.V.M., *The Holistic Veterinary Approach to Healthy Pets*, Total Health, June 1996

•Kozlenko, Richard, DPM, Ph.D. MPH, Henson, Ronald H., *Latest Scientific Research on Spirulina: Effects on the AIDS Virus, Cancer and the Immune System*, 1996

•Leviton, Richard, *A Shot In The Dark*, Yoga Journal, May/June 1992

•Long, Cheryl Fritz, *Household Hazards, Protecting your pets from poisons*, Better Homes and Gardens, August 1992

•McCrea, Bruce, *Boswella*, Natural Pet, March/April, 1996

•McGinnis, T., *The Well Cat Book. The Classic Comprehensive Handbook of Cat Care.*, Random House, 1993

•McHattie, Grace, Your Cat Naturally, Carroll & Graf Pub., 1992

•McKay, Pat, *Reigning Cats & Dogs*, Oscar Pub., 1992

•McKay, Pat, *Have You and Your Animals Had Your Oxygen Today?*, Natural Pet, Jan/Feb., 1996

•Mendola, Kathleen Finn, *The Nutritional Value of Green Foods*, NFM's Nutrition Science News, Dec. 1996

•Moskowitz, M.D., *The Case Against Immunizations,* Journal of the American Institute of Homeopathy, National. Center for Homeopathy

•Murray, Michael T. N.D., *The Healing Power of Foods,* Prima Pub. 1993.

•*Nutrition*, Dog World, p. 25, Aug. 1994

•Olarsch, I. Gerald, N.D., *Why Minerals are so vital to Pet Health*, Natural Pet p.22. Jan/Feb 1996

•Pavia, Audry, *The Right Combinations*, Natural Pet Jul/Aug 1996

•Pitcairn, R.H., Pitcairn, S.H., *Natural Health for Dogs and Cats*, Rodale Press, 1982

•Quershi, M.A., Ali, R.A., *Spirulina platensis Exposure Enhances Macrophage Phagocytic Function In Cats,* Immunopharmacology and Immunotoxicology, 1996

•Rhodes, John, *Light, Radiation and Pet Health*, Natural Pet, May-June, 1995

•Santillo, Humbart MH, N.D., *Food Enzymes*, Holm Press, 1993.

•Seibold, R., *Cereal Grass: What's in it for You?*, Lawrence, KS: Wilderness Community Education Foundation, 1990

•*Shedding Light on "Lite" Food,* Tufts University School of Veterinary Medicine Catnip Newsletter, Vol 4, No. 8, Nov. 1996

•Silver, Robert J., DVM, MS, *Protecting Your Animal Friend From the Toxic Environment,* Natural Pet, Nov.-Dec. 1995

•Silver, Robert, J. DVM, MS, *Natural Approaches to Pet Health*, Lecture, Natural Products Expo, Sept., 1995

•Smith, Bob L., *Organic Foods vs Supermarket Foods: Element Levels* Journal of Applied Nutrition, Vol 45, No 1,1993, pp. 35-39.

•Smith, Charlene, *Green Foods,* Natural Pet, May/June 1994

•Somer, Elizabeth M.A., R.D. *The Essential Guide to Vitamins and Minerals*, Harper-Collins Pub., 1992.

•*"Source" is Best for Seaweed*, Michael Plumb's Horse Journal, Vol 3, Number 4

•Stein, Diane, *The Natural Remedy Book for Dogs & Cats*, The Crossing Press, 1994

•Steinberg, Phillip N., C.N.C., *Cat's Claw, Amazing Herbal Medicine from the Amazon*, Natural Pet, p. 34, Jan/Feb 1996

•Stockton, Susan, M.A., CRC, *Aluminum Toxicity in Animals*, Pet Trader, August 1995

APPENDIX A

TACHYONIZED PRODUCTS. Tachyon energy, otherwise known as life force energy, is not a specific nutrient, yet it has been proven to have an integral part in the healing realm (see Chapter 1). **Tachyonized Water** is simple to administer. (Applying 2-15 drops directly into pet's mouth 2-3 time/day or sprinkle it onto their moist food.) **Tachyonized Silica Gel** has helped pets suffering from ill health, arthritis, hip dysplasia and pain. (Dosage: 2 drops on their food a.m. and p.m.). **Life Capsule** is a pendant filled with minute Tachyonized cells which are constantly attracting the balancing life force energy into your pet. (LC-M designed for pets 20# or less; LC-L for larger animals; Pooch Pouch for horses and livestock.) ADVANCED TACHYON TECHNOLOGIES, 480 Tesconi Circle, Santa Rosa CA 95401   (800) 966-9341 email: tachyon@tachyon-energy.com www. tachyon-energy.com

PREMIUM LINE OF ALL NATURAL PET PRODUCTS. Ark Naturals Products for Pets™ manufactures a premium line of all-natural pet care and pet health products. **Ark Naturals Products for Pets**™ formulates products that cover both sides of animal health...wellness and remedy. All **Ark**™ products are formulated by our team of veterinarians and biochemists and use all human, pharmaceutical-grade raw materials. **Ark**™ wellness products are formulated to boost your pet's immune system and provides all vitamins, minerals, amino acids and nutrients not available in commercial pet foods—even premium foods. **Ark**™ remedy products target specific issues and will help to alleviate and relieve conditions such as: stress and nervous behavior; joint issues and arthritis; flea, tick and biting insect problems; ear and eye problems; dry skin and digestion related problems. **Ark Naturals Products for Pets**™ offers pet guardians their best opportunity to take a proactive approach to ensure their pet's good health and general well-being. All of our products are environmentally friendly, human-grade and veterinarian recommended. ARK NATURALS PRODUCTS FOR PETS™, 6166 Taylor Road #105, Naples, FL 34109 (941) 592-9388 Fax (941) 592-9338 email:sales@arknaturals.com   www.arknaturals.com

AIR PURIFICATION SYSTEMS. Alpine Air Purifiers provide the most advanced technology for treating indoor air pollution using a combination of ionization and oxidation, utilizing solid state electronics. The ionization process removes particulate from the air including pet dander, dust, allergens, and airborne matter by causing it to settle out of the air. In addition, negative ions relax the animals. A controlled ozone system removes all organic odors and kills bacteria and viruses. There are no filters to replace and maintenance is minimal. The Alpine machines are used and recommended by veterinarians, breeders, groomers, animal shelters and boarding kennels. For a free consultation, call ALPINE AIR, 220 Reservoir St., Needham Heights, MA 02494 (800) 628-2209

HUMAN EDIBLE, WHOLE FOODS SUPPLEMENT. The Missing Link® **SuperSupplement** for dogs, cats and horses is made with human edible, whole foods and food concentrates by special methods that stabilize the good fats, enzymes, vitamins and friendly bacteria ingredients necessary for optimum health. Users report a wide range of positive results, including relief of excessive shedding, dry skin, hot spots, doggy odor, stinky ears, wet drippy eyes, allergies, digestive problems and joint stiffness and pain. Energy levels increase in older animals, cats stop throwing up hairballs, feline acne disappears. Horses' coats develop a "spit n' shine polish, they get less joint swelling and pain, less respiratory distress, more calm, less founder and less sand colic. Animals swell less after surgery and heal faster. DESIGNING HEALTH INC., 28310 Avenue Crocker, Unit G, Valencia CA 91355 (800) 774-7387 Fax (661) 257-0158, email:sales@designinghealth.com   www.designinghealth.com

HOMEOPATHIC MEDICINES AND NUTRITIONAL SUPPLEMENTS. For ten years, **Dr. Goodpet** has offered dog and cat owners proven homeopathic medicines that work without side effects. They are beneficial against fleas, insect bites, scratching, stress and motion sickness, diarrhea, bad breath, ear and eye problems and now arthritis. Vitamin and mineral supplements are also available for very young animals, adults and seniors. Canine and feline digestive enzymes aid the digestive process. **Dr. Goodpet PURE** shampoo is hypoallergenic, gentle and nourishing for skin. New to the line is boric acid carpet treatment for fleas, beneficial nematodes for yard fleas, a 100% vitamin C product and **"Hot Pants"**, a stain control garment for puppy "mistakes", bladder control problems, and dogs in heat. DR. GOODPET, Inglewood, CA (800)-222-9932

COMPLETE LINE OF HOLISTIC PRODUCTS. Dynamite® Specialty Products has been in the animal nutrition business under ownership of the same family since 1933, offering nutritional counseling and **holistic products**. Their complete line of holistic products enhances the health and well being of dogs, cats, horses, birds, ferrets, and all other exotic animals, humans and plants. These include chelated mineral formulas, pure Ester C®, digestive aids, detoxifiers, topicals, homeopathics, all-natural shampoo and insect repellents, premium naturally-preserved foods, colloidal fertilizers and more. Used by top kennels, stables and pet owners, this company has distributor opportunities available in addition to retail product sales. DYNAMITE® SPECIALTY PRODUCTS, 310 East Watertower Lane, Meridian, ID 83642-6283 (800) 677-0919 www.dynamiteonline.com

ENZYME SUPPLEMENTS FOR NUTRITION, COATS AND JOINTS. Enzyme supplementation will help your pet gain more nutrition from any diet. You'll see the results in more energy, better coat and lower foods bills. **Pet-Zimes**™ (available through Enzymes, Inc.), include a general digestive formula and **Peppy Pet**™, a special joint support blend. **Vet-Zimes**™ (available through your veterinarian), provide specific therapeutic potency products for dogs and cats. For more information, or to order: (800) 647-6377 email: marketing@enzymesinc.com ENZYMES, INC., 8500 NW River Park Dr., #227, Parkville, MO 64152

DEER VELVET ANTLER. This product has been shown in studies, to substantially benefit animals suffering from stress, muscle and joint related problems as well as skin conditions, when taken regularly. It increases pet energy and stamina and improves kidney and liver function. **Velvet Antler** is composed primarily of protein, with collagen as the major protein, as well as essential minerals. It is a superior natural powerhouse of nutrients including: amino acids, hematopoietin, glucosamines, chondroitin sulfate, anti-inflammatory prostaglandins, growth hormone complex, and erythropoietin. Pure **Velvet Antler** is a gentle, safe and natural supplement for all mammals. GOLD MOUNTAIN TRADING COMPANY, LTD., P.O. Box 267, Katikati, New Zealand +645-549-3492   www.PureVelvetAntler.com

SUPER GREEN NUTRITION FOR PETS. Great tasting **Barley Dog**™ and **Barley Cat**™ are the original "green" supplements made from barley grass juice(grown without pesticides or chemical fertilizers), garlic, brown rice and a vegetarian-source nutritional yeast with a bacon-like flavor. Barley Cat™ also includes taurine and chicken liver. Provides active enzymes, vitamins C & E, beta-carotene, amino acids, chlorophyll, proteins and essential trace minerals to promote healthy skin and coat, reduce bad breath, improve digestion and restore energy levels - especially among senior animals. Sold in pet and health-food stores or by mail order. Questions, comments or ordering information, please call GREEN FOODS CORPORATION, (800) 777-4430.

CHINESE HERBAL FORMULAS. Since 1989 Herb-cetera has helped develop and manufacture the 1st and most comprehensive line of Chinese Herbal formulas for pets, using only the freshest and most effective herbs available in Traditional Chinese Medicine. They are completely natural, safe, effective and in powder form to be added to your pet's wet food. Clinically tested by the Healing Oasis Veterinarian Hospital since its inception, these formulas have a proven track record of outstanding results with no side effects. **Pet Therapy's** line of formulas include: **Crystal Clear** for prevention of urinary tract infections and stones as well a elimination of stones with pain and bleeding. **Expel** a natural dewormer; **Calm & Easy** for anxiety and nervous behavior; **Pain Free** to alleviate most pain, especially from arthritis; **Replenish** to restore wellness after surgery or illness; **Recovery** to help eliminate accumulations such as tumors, cysts, etc. Herb-cetera, New Britain, CT, Distributed by HOLISTIC PET MEDIC, (860) 832-8999 www.herbworld.com/herbschool

ESSENTIAL FATTY ACID SUPPLEMENT. This formula replenishes Essential Fatty Acids destroyed by temperature necessary to cook and process food. **Animal Essentials** contains Lecithin, Sea Bed Trace Minerals, Spirulina plus Marine Lipids and comes in a fish shaped capsule (for cats, you can snip off the tail and squeeze out the contents). **Multi-vitamin Herbal Supplement** contains Herbs, Mineral Chelates, Vitamins, Spirulina and Lecithin, in a base of stabilized flaxseed which a great source of Omega-3. Also available is **Green Alternative**, 100% certified organic, rich is antioxidants, vitamins and minerals. If used as directed, these supplements will increase your pet's own immune system and its own healing powers. These formulas are made with all natural (human grade only) ingredients. They are safe, effective and easy to use. MERRITT NATURALS™, P.O. Box 532, Rumson, NJ 07760 (888) 463-7748 www.animalessentials.com

FLOWER REMEDIES. Safe treatments to help emotional issues pets may develop. **First Aid Remedy** can be used in any emergency situation. In times of extreme stress or crisis such as accidents, injuries or insect or animal bites, a few drops given to your pet will provide immediate relief. It will help to calm your pet and promote fast healing of injury, trauma, or pain. (Works equally well for humans.) **Fearfulness** helps animals cope with situations such as illness, loneliness and aging. It also reduces panic and terror when an animal has been attacked. **Grief/Loss** is useful when a member of the family (human or animal) has left home permanently or the pet's situation has changed drastically. **Jealousy/ Competitiveness** works beautifully in cases of behavioral difficulties between pets and/or their owners. NATURAL LABS, P.O. Box 5351, Lake Montezuma, AZ 86342 (800) 233-0810 Fax (520) 567-7534   www.alternatehealth.net

CRYSTALLOID MINERALS (electrolytes) FOR BODY AND SKIN. Trace minerals in crystalloid form allow for greater cellular absorption. They are the key to shiny, healthy fur, good calcium absorption and a healthy disposition. **PetLyte**™ puts the life force back in food and water to fortify the body's defense against chemical additives. It is a liquid blend of trace minerals in an electrolyte base **Skin-Aide**™ is the first pet skin healing and nutrient spray for relief from itchy and patchy skin, infections, fungus, and to promote thicker, shiny coats on all animals. Due to its crystalloid nature, its penetrates rapidly to the deepest skin layers with minerals and a unique blend of ionically-bound herbs. Also available: A unique broad scope, whole food supplement uses a European slow extraction "cracked cell" yeast-culture process grown specifically for animal consumption. **Pet Total-Lyte™** is exceptionally high in protein, which is further enhanced by the addition of electrolytes into the yeast. Protein cannot be utilized by the body unless a minimal amount of trace minerals (electrolytes) are present. The production of enzymes cannot take place without the body's electrolytes. Combined with the liquid mineral, Pet-Lyte,™ this protein supplement is readily absorbed and utilized. NATURE'S PATH., P.O. Box 7862, North Port, FL 34287 (800) 326-5772

HOMEOPATHIC DETOXIFIERS & HEALING SYSTEM. Healing animals is simple, safe and effective with homeopathic medicine. The **Newton for Pets P25 Detoxifier** assists your pet with removing harmful metabolic and environmental toxins. This formula promotes general body cleansing to speed the healing process and maintain good health and can be combined with other formulas to safely treat many common ailments that affect animals today. These may include skin problems, digestive difficulties, arthritis, nervousness, cough and much more! It is possible to help animals get well without the lingering side-effects of synthetic chemical drugs. The Detoxifier is available for people too. NEWTON LABORATORIES, INC., 2360 Rockaway Industrial Blvd., Conyers, GA 30012 (800) 448-7256 email: mailinfo@newtonlabs.net www.newtonlabs.net

RAW ENZYMES/VITAMINS IN A GRAVY MIX. NUPRO users have had wonderful results with pets who have allergies, hot spots, arthritis, poor appetite, anemia, scratching and itching. This gravy forming mix (liver base) includes bee pollen, flaxseed, borage seed, lecithin, garlic, acidophilus, Norwegian kelp, nutritional yeast, garlic. It has no ash, sugar, fillers, preservatives or by-products and is highly recommended by many healthy pets. For cats the same supplement is available as **Nupro Health Nuggets.** Their **Custom Electrolyte Formula** with balanced ratios of all minerals essential for optimum health, helps to prevent dehydration and muscle tie-ups, maintains proper fluid balance in the blood and tissues, stabilizes energy levels, combats fatigue, nausea, diarrhea and upset stomach and is good for nervous puppies and kittens. Also available: **Nupro Joint Support** with added Glucosamine complex, MSM and vitamin C. NUTRI-PET RESEARCH, INC. 8 W. Main St., Farmingdale, NJ 07727 (800) 360-3300, (732) 938-2233 email: nupro@skyweb.net   www.nuprosupplements.com

OMEGA 3 WITHOUT FISH OIL. Essential fatty acids (Omega 3 & 6) are the building blocks of cell membranes and will help balance and normalize the body. Since they are processed out of most of our foods, we must use supplements. **FORTIFIED FLAX** provides these essential fatty acids with the oil in flaxseed. It is nature's richest source of Omega-3 and this ground whole flaxseed also contains all essential amino acids, high fiber, complex carbohydrates, vitamins and minerals. This necessary supplement comes in meal form, and therefore is easy to sprinkle on or mix into your pet's food. OMEGA-LIFE, Inc., P.O. Box 208, Brookfield WI 53008-0208 (800) EAT-FLAX (328-3529).

DENTAL CARE AND HEALTHY PRODUCTS. Dental calculus buildup weakens teeth and gums and can lead to other health problems. Pet Central offers **Greenies**, the Lean Green Dental Machine, as a nutritional dental aid. Greenies are clinically proven to reduce dental calculus buildup by 87%. Designed as a fully digestible chew bone, Greenies are made with human-grade ingredients and do not contain any inert materials, artificial flavors, colors or preservatives. Dental benefits include plaque removal, tooth and gum enhancement, odor reduction. Also available are KR products for supplemental, preventive and holistric treatment of conditions: **InflamAway** contains glucosamine and yucca to reduce joint swelling and antioxidants to flush impurities; **Super Oxy Green** neutralizes harmful free-radicals and provides nutritional support for pets with arthritis, stress and allergies; **Comple-Zyme** can be combined with Super Oxy Green to help reduce body odors and digestive problems. **MaxiDerm and MaxiDerm EFA** relieve skin conditions and provides essential fatty acids to maintain a healthy coat and skin; PET CENTRAL, 6100 Monroe St, Sylvania, OH 43560 (888) 892-7393

CEREAL GRASS SUPPLEMENTS. Natural, whole food supplements are necessary for proper nutritional balance. Many processed pet foods are lacking the same nutrients found in **Pines Wheat Grass,** such as anti-oxidants, chlorophyll, fiber, vitamins and minerals. **Pines Wheat Grass** nutritionally resembles a dark green leafy vegetable and helps balance the high acidity, all-protein diet of most pets. The naturally occurring nutrition in **Pines Wheat Grass** should be a part of your pet's daily diet. PINES INTERNATIONAL, P.O. Box 1107, Lawrence, KS 66044 (800) 697-4637 Canada (888) 436-6697   www.wheatgrass.com

HIP AND JOINT SUPPORT. Winston's Joint Formula was developed after extensive research and consultations with professional and holistic practitioners. It proved to be so effective at relieving symptoms of degenerative joint disorders, such as arthritis, hip dysplasia, osteochondrosis (OCD), ankle and joint problems, and growing pains, that the Pet Project was formed to offer it to other pet owners. **Winston's Joint Formula** contains only pure and potent natural food supplements from very reputable processors. We have seen dramatic improvements in mobility with noticeable relief from pain. Testimonials and more information is available through us directly and on the Internet. THE PET PROJECT, 269 S. Beverly Drive #321, Beverly Hills, CA 90212 (323) 466-1205 (or call (860) 824-5301 for the latest number) email: samf@icnt.net   www.cyberark.com/animal/winston.htm

ALL-NATURAL HIGH POTENCY DIGESTIVE ENZYMES. PROZYME™ is a highly concentrated blend of the most potent plant derived enzymes available for improving digestion. **PROZYME's** proprietary blend is unique, and the formula is stomach acid stable. **PROZYME** is scientifically proven to increase the absorption of vital nutrients and essential fatty acids, especially zinc, selenium, vitamin B_6, EPA (omega 3) and linoleic acid from your pet's food, and supplements by up to 71%. Unlocking the nutrients and getting them absorbed and utilized by the body is beneficial for animals of all ages, especially older ones or pregnant/nursing ones, and those experiencing allergies, digestive or immune disorders, excessive shedding, skin or haircoat problems, joint difficulties, flatulence, lethargy, bloating, and coprophagian or hairballs. Backed by over 20 years of field use, research, and published studies substantiating its effectiveness, **PROZYME** is beneficial and safe for dogs and cats. PROZYME PRODUCTS, 6444 N. Ridgeway Ave., Lincolnwood, IL 60712 (800) 522-5537 Fax (847) 982-1310

MAGNETS AND PETS. Magnet Therapy Pet Collars are made from all-natural magnets. As seen on TV. See page 76 for benefits of the use of magnets. THE GEM STEM, INC., P.O. Box 6112, Delray Beach, FL 33484 (561) 276-5292

SEAWEEDS AND MICRONUTRIENTS FOR DOGS. Micronutrient deficiencies in foods are more prevalent from years of soil depletion and processing of food ingredients. Symptoms of micronutrient deficiencies include coat, skin and allergy problems, breeding and growth difficulties, weakened immune systems and general lack of thriftiness.*(see page 65 for details)* The **SOURCE®** products supply a broad spectrum of concentrated, all-natural micronutrients derived from nature's richest storehouse, the ocean's seaweeds. As a direct processor of seaweed meal ingredients (not just a re-labeler), SOURCE, INC., has been able to develop unique harvesting and processing techniques that maximize bio-availability and result in the most potent and effective micronutrient nutritional aids available. **SOURCE®** the original maintenance formula, is beneficial for all breeds and ages. SOURCE PLUS! Contains added natural ingredients of particular help for dogs suffering from coat, skin, allergy, breeding and growth problems. SOURCE, INC., 101 Fowler Rd., N. Branford, CT 06471 (800) 232-2365   www.4source.com

FLOWER REMEDIES JUST FOR PETS. A line of flower remedies specifically for pets has been designed by Kelvin Levitt, R.Ph., a registered pharmacist for over 30 years and health food store owner for 20 years. Using customized formulas in conjunction with Deva (*see Natural Labs in this listing*) and other producers, he has created a line that treats the emotional issues as outlined in this book. These remedies provide help for pets without resorting to the use of drugs and their associated side-effects. For more information and a complementary audio-tape contact: TODAY WHOLISTIC CONSULTANTS, 2219 Arden Rd., Baltimore, MD 21209 (410) 664-0620 email: klevitt@mindspring.com

SPECIALTY FORMULATIONS FOR DOGS, CATS, BIRDS. Vetri-Science offers specialty nutritional formulations: for immune problems resulting in skin problems (**Vetri-Liquid DMG, Vetri-DMG Tablets**); allergies (Antiox); anti-stress nutrients (**Vetri-Liquid-DMG, Vetri-DMG Tablets**); connective tissue support (**Glyco-Flex, Glyco-Flex Plus, Glyco-Flex Plus DS, Nu-Cat, Cell-Advance, Multi-Source Glucosamine, Single-Source Glucosamine, Vetri-Disc,**); antioxidants (**Cell-Advance, Antiox**); vomiting and diarrhea support (**Acetylator**); periodontal and cardiovascular support (**Co-Q10**); shark cartilage (**Vetri-Shark**) and multiple vitamin and mineral formulations (**Nu-Cat, Canine Plus**). Ask your vet for these products. VETRI-SCIENCE LABORATORIES, 20 New England Dr., Essex Junction, VT 05453 (800) 882-9993.

GARLIC EXTRACT. .More than 100 scientific studies have confirmed the safety and efficacy of the world's only truly odorless garlic. **KYOLIC**® **AGED GARLIC EXTRACT's**™ unique aging process brings out safer, more valuable and effective components than those in fresh raw garlic. Only **KYOLIC**® has anti-viral properties and anti-cancer activity, is truly a cell protector and helps activate the Phase II detoxifying enzymes system. **KYO-GREEN,**® an energy booster and power drink, is a pleasant tasting alkalizing green powder beverage in a food form, that puts the immune system into "over drive." It is a blend of organically grown cereal grasses (barley & wheat), Bulgarian chlorella, kelp and brown rice, full of natural vitamins, minerals and enzymes. **KYO-DOPHILUS**® and **PROBIATA,** two potent "Probiotics" necessary for optimum colon health, never need refrigeration, are heat stable, are pre-adapted to the colon and re-establish the friendly flora damaged by antibiotics and poor diet. WAKUNAGA OF AMERICA, CO., LTD., 23501 Madero, Mission Viejo, CA 92691 (800) 825-7888

A LITTLE BIT OF EVERYTHING. Chemical free living is what every pet hopes their owner will give them. The **Whiskers mail order catalog** and store offers a multitude of natural and holistic products from food to frisbees, halters to homeopathy and everything in between. They are dedicated to providing you with safe, non-toxic alternatives to the products you may currently be using. For a free catalog call WHISKERS, 235 E 9th St., New York, NY 10003 (800) 944-7537 or (212)-979-2532 Web: http://choicemall.com/ whiskers

WORLD'S BEST CAT LITTER. World's Best Cat Litter® is an all-natural, 99% dust-free clumping cat litter made of whole-kernel corn. It has excellent odor control, is easy to use and is safe for you, your pets and the environment. The micro-cellular structure absorbs odors without any synthetic chemicals, perfumes, deodorants or scented oils. Clumps are compact and firm so you just scoop and flush to keep your home clean and fresh smelling. Cats love the texture and particle size. WORLD'S BEST CAT LITTER, 1600 Oregon St., Muscatine, IA 52761 (877) 367-9225 (FOR-WBCL)   www.worldsbestcatlitter.com

OTHER BOOKS FROM SAFE GOODS

· A Guide To A Naturally Healthy Bird	$ 9.95
· A.D.D. The Natural Approach	$ 4.95
· The Brain Train	$ 4.95
· El Método Natural (A.D.D., The Natural Approach Spanish)	$ 6.95
· The Secrets of Staying Young	$ 9.95
· All Natural Anti-Aging Skin Care	$ 4.95
· Feeling Younger with Homeopathic HGH	$ 7.95
· The Humorous Herbalist	$14.95
· Plant Power	$19.95
· Effective Natural Stress & Weight Management	$ 8.95
· Natural Solutions for Sexual Enhancement	$ 9.95
· The High Performance Diet	$ 7.95
· The Backseat Flyer	$ 9.95
· Nutritional Leverage for Great Golf	$ 9.95
· The New Thin You	$ 9.95
· Chronic Fatigue Syndrome for the Modern Woman	$ 9.95
· Pycnogenol®, The Bark with the Bite	$ 8.95
· Curing Allergies with Visual Imagery	$14.95
· Eliminating Pilot Error	$ 7.95
· Audio tapes:	
ADD, The Natural Approach	$ 9.95
Crystalloid Electrolytes, your body's energy source	$ 9.95
· Videos:	
Your Child and ADD	$29.95
Human Factors and Pilot Error	$19.95

ORDER LINE (888)-NATURE-1, credit cards accepted
Shipping: $4.00 each book
Safe Goods
PO Box 36
E. Canaan, CT 06024
(860) 824-5301
website: safegoodspub.com